PREPARE FOR IELTS
GENERAL TRAINING PRACTICE TESTS

Penny Cameron and Vanessa Todd

UNIVERSITY OF
TECHNOLOGY SYDNEY

INSEARCH
Level 2, 187 Thomas Street
Sydney NSW 2000 Australia
www.insearch.edu.au

International Office
University of Technology, Sydney
Broadway NSW 2007 Australia
www.uts.edu.au

Copyright © 2006 INSEARCH Limited

First published 2001
Reprinted with corrections 2002
Second edition 2005
Reprinted with corrections 2006

The publisher would like to thank Mary Jane Hogan for her contribution to the earlier editions of this book.

National Library of Australia
Cataloguing-in-Publication data

Cameron, Penny
Prepare for IELTS: General Training Practice Tests

ISBN 0-908537-24-7

1.International English Language Testing System
2.English language—Examinations, questions, etc
3.English language—Textbooks for foreign speakers

I.Cameron, Penny
II.Insearch UTS
III.University of Technology, Sydney. International Office.
IV. Title
V.Title: Prepare for International English Language Testing System
VI.Title: Prepare for IELTS

Publications Manager	Renée Rimington
Consultants	David Larbalestier and Anna Shymkiw
Book Design	Stuart Gibson, Book Design Australia, www.bookdesign.com.au
Cover Design	EKH Branding House, www.ekhbranding.com.au
Line Illustrations	Pam Horsnell
Diagrams	Stuart Gibson and Simon Leong
Photography	iStockPhoto
Print Production	SNP Security Printing Pte Ltd, www.snpcorp.com

2006 Edition Corrections by Kathleen Chew

INSEARCH
ENGLISH

PREPARE FOR IELTS
GENERAL TRAINING PRACTICE TESTS

UNIVERSITY OF
TECHNOLOGY SYDNEY

INSEARCH
ENGLISH

CONTENTS

WHY CHOOSE

→ **NEW!** Updated with the new 2006 writing rubrics

→ Developed by **IELTS experts**

→ **NEW!** Includes **5 Sample** speaking interviews on CD

→ Covers all four parts of the IELTS test
LISTENING, READING, WRITING and **SPEAKING**

→ **NEW!** Includes **BONUS** reading material to help you prepare!

→ All tasks have been comprehensively tested in the classroom

→ Practical **hints** and **tips**

→ Logical layout with clear explanations (Now in colour!)

THIS SERIES?

→ Relevant information and tasks

→ Full **answer key** and **transcripts**

→ **NEW!** Sample writing answers

→ A comprehensive **variety** of question types

"As I knew that IELTS is a fairly difficult test, I was a bit worried about the strategies I had to know in order to be successful. Speaking English is one thing, but the other is knowing how to tackle the test itself."

FILIP ZAHRADNIK, SLOVAKIA

NEW:DIRECTION

Proudly published by

INSEARCH
ENGLISH

INSEARCH PROVIDES COURSES THAT LEAD TO UNIVERSITY DEGREES AND OTHER QUALIFICATIONS ACROSS A BROAD RANGE OF DISCIPLINES

→ As the provider of innovative language and academic pathways to university studies, INSEARCH is a leading institution of its type and teaching English is the cornerstone of its success. INSEARCH has a history of expertise in IELTS preparation, both within Australia and through its global network.

AUSTRALIA

→ Located in central Sydney, INSEARCH offers a wide range of IELTS preparation courses to suit different needs and is the provider of academic pathways to the University of Technology Sydney (UTS), one of the largest IELTS test centres in the world.

VIETNAM

→ INSEARCH operates the Australian Centre for Education and Training with joint venture partner, IDP Education Australia. A wide range of IELTS preparation courses, including customised corporate courses, are offered at both the Hanoi and Ho Chi Minh City locations. Both centres also offer pathway courses to IELTS. This option allows students not ready to sit the IELTS test to receive more preparatory tuition and optimise their preparation time.

→ IDP Education Australia is an approved IELTS test centre in both Hanoi and Ho Chi Minh City.

INDONESIA

→ The Australia Centre Medan is operated by INSEARCH. The centre offers a variety of English courses, including IELTS preparation, and is also an IELTS test centre.

THAILAND

→ INSEARCH operates the Australia Centre Chiang Mai where candidates may enrol in IELTS preparation courses and, as an approved IELTS test centre, may also register for and sit the IELTS test.

CHINA

→ INSEARCH also operates the Sydney Institute of Language of Commerce (SILC) in partnership with, and on the three campuses of, Shanghai University. SILC offers academic English preparation courses as well as diplomas in business and commerce, IT and communication.

UNITED KINGDOM

→ INSEARCH offers a range of English language courses and provides accredited academic pathway courses for entry into the second year of study (business and computer science) at University of Essex.

courses@insearch.edu.au

www.insearch.edu.au

CRICOS provider code: 00859D

UTS: SYDNEY'S CITY UNIVERSITY

SYDNEY'S CITY UNIVERSITY, THE UNIVERSITY OF TECHNOLOGY, SYDNEY (UTS) REFLECTS THE CITY AROUND IT: MODERN, DIVERSE AND PROGRESSIVE.

Proudly published by

UNIVERSITY OF
TECHNOLOGY SYDNEY

→ BUSINESS
→ DESIGN, ARCHITECTURE AND BUILDING
→ EDUCATION
→ ENGINEERING
→ HUMANITIES AND SOCIAL SCIENCES
→ INFORMATION TECHNOLOGY
→ LAW
→ NURSING, MIDWIFERY AND HEALTH
→ SCIENCE
→ INTERNATIONAL STUDIES

→ Delivering professionally focused courses and
topical research, UTS offers practical education
with an international perspective. It is this
unique combination of practicality, international
awareness, and city culture which distinguishes
UTS from other universities. Offering more than
100 undergraduate and 200 postgraduate courses,
UTS is much more than a technical university.

→ As one of Australia's largest and most respected
universities, UTS attracts students from all
over the world. The University encourages
international interaction, fostering worldwide
student exchanges and partnerships with over 110
universities in 24 countries. A multicultural mix of
more than 30,000 students, including over 6,000
international students from 115 countries have
chosen UTS because it offers:

→ CAREER-RELEVANT EDUCATION
→ TEACHING EXCELLENCE
→ A DIVERSE RANGE OF COURSES
→ EXCELLENT GRADUATE OUTCOMES
→ A MULTICULTURAL MIX OF STUDENTS
→ EXCELLENT FACILITIES AND STUDENT SERVICES
→ A UNIQUE EXPERIENCE OF AUSTRALIA

international@uts.edu.au
www.uts.edu.au/international/

CRICOS provider code: 00099F

INTRODUCTION

THE IELTS TEST

ABOUT THE IELTS TEST

The International English Language Testing System (IELTS) was introduced in 1989 to help universities and colleges assess the English skills of applicants wishing to study or train in the English language. It continues to be used for this purpose and is also used as a general test of English for immigration and employment in many countries.

Candidates must choose to sit either the **Academic** or the **General Training** IELTS test.

▷ The **Academic** IELTS test is for individuals who plan to study in English at university (undergraduate or postgraduate level), and is designed to test the understanding and use of complex academic language.

▷ The **General Training** IELTS test is suitable for individuals requiring a more general level of English proficiency for college, high school, employment or immigration purposes.

The IELTS test is divided into four sections: **Listening, Reading, Writing** and **Speaking.**

All candidates sit the same **Listening** and **Speaking** test. However, **Academic** and **General Training** candidates each sit a different **Reading** and **Writing** test. Detailed information on each test is provided at the beginning of each unit in this book.

THE TEST FORMAT

30 minutes	**Listening** Test
60 minutes	Academic **Reading** Test _or_ General Training **Reading** Test
60 minutes	Academic **Writing** Test _or_ General Training **Writing** Test
11-14 minutes	**Speaking** Test

There is no pass or fail mark in the IELTS test. Candidates are marked on a band scale of 1 to 9 in each part of the test. These bands classify a candidate's ability to use and understand English in particular contexts, and correspond approximately to the categories of English proficiency as listed below.

Band 9	**Expert User**
Band 8	**Very Good User**
Band 7	**Good User**
Band 6	**Competent User**
Band 5	**Modest User**
Band 4	**Limited User**
Band 3	**Extremely Limited User**
Band 2	**Intermittent User**
Band 1	**Non User**
Band 0	**No Original English Used**

The Test Results Form (TRF) contains a score for each part of the test as well as an average (overall) band score.

Depending on various English language requirements, individual universities, organisations and countries decide which IELTS band score is suitable for their applicants.

For more information on IELTS you can visit the IELTS website at www.ielts.org or ask your IELTS centre for a copy of *The IELTS Handbook*.

INTRODUCTION

IMPROVEMENT **TIPS**

Candidates may sit the IELTS test as many times as they wish, and from 1 May 2006 do not need to wait 90 days before taking it again. However, it should be understood that the average learner requires approximately 400 hours of instruction and study to progress just one band level in IELTS.

Before sitting the test it is important and helpful to:

1 Familiarise yourself with the test **FORMAT** (page 13)   **F**

2 Improve your **TEST** skills with practice tests (page 14)   **T**

3 **USE** your English skills every day (page 15)   **U**

Many candidates enrol in an IELTS Preparation Course at a language school to help them prepare fully for the test. Combined with independent study, and daily practice using the English language, a preparation course will help candidates achieve their target band score. (See page 16 for an overview of what an IELTS course will usually cover.)

F

An important part of preparing for the IELTS test is understanding the test structure. What are the sections of the test? Which section comes first? Second? How much time is allowed for each section? How many questions are there? How long must I speak for?

▷ Familiarise yourself with the question types used. There are many different types of questions, and they do not all appear in each test version. However, knowing different question types will save you time because you'll interpret the questions in the test more easily.

Once you are familiar with the test format, you will be more relaxed. You can focus on answering the questions rather than worrying about how many questions there are or how much time you have left.

IMPROVEMENT **TIPS**

Effective test skills will best demonstrate your language skills during the short examination time.

▷ The first skill to practise is timing. You should practise reading and writing under time constraints. Try speed reading every day. Read short passages in a fixed time (for example, set yourself three minutes to read the passage quickly). You will not understand everything in the first reading but you will become more familiar with skimming a text to get a general idea of its main points. You can then return to the text later to pay more attention to certain parts.

▷ Similarly, try writing for a set period of time every day. For this exercise, total accuracy is not necessary; rather, you are practising getting your ideas down on paper quickly. Set yourself a different topic each day (such as computers, family, different countries etc), and write as much as you can for five minutes. Write notes to your friends or short descriptions of something you have seen. Your speed will improve gradually, and this will be very useful in the test when you must write a certain number of words for each task in a set period of time.

▷ Start with the tests in this book. Complete each under test conditions then afterwards look at them again. What type of questions were asked in each section? Multiple choice? Short answers? Matching parts of sentences? Filling in diagrams? Think about the kinds of questions and what they are asking you to do. If you had problems with any, do them again, slowly, so that you are sure of what you are doing.

▷ Always read the test questions carefully. Do not assume that they will be exactly the same as the practice tests!

You might like to sit a real IELTS test "just for practice". You will get to know how it works, and can practise working under test conditions. Then, when you are ready to take the IELTS test, you will be familiar with the format and will have already practised your test skills.

If this is not possible, ask other students who have already taken the IELTS test about their experience. Find out which tasks they think require the most preparation.

This is where the hard work lies. Test practice and knowing the format will help you in the IELTS test by leaving you free to concentrate on your language skills. However, you will need to work hard to improve these skills.

The IELTS test measures the extent to which candidates possess the language skills needed for study, employment or everyday life. For this reason it includes tasks that might be found in real-life situations. Therefore, you will not be able to simply memorise answers. Your IELTS score will reflect your language ability and how you apply it to certain situations.

▷ If you enrol in an IELTS Preparation Course your teacher will introduce and extend a range of skills such as those highlighted on page 16.

▷ If you do not enrol in an IELTS Preparation Course you should try to immerse yourself in the English language. Most experts agree that this is the quickest way to improve.

This may be difficult if you live in a non-English speaking country. However, try to find English interest groups, go to English films, listen to English on the radio, join an online chat room and read English books and magazines.

In an English speaking country this is much easier. Try to spend as much of your day as possible using English. You will probably end up dreaming in English too!

GENERAL AREAS COVERED BY AN IELTS PREPARATION COURSE

LISTENING

▷ Practising all question types

▷ Recognising intonation patterns (questions, surprise etc)

▷ Varieties of spoken English, including Australian, British, North American and New Zealand

▷ Listening for specific information, keywords, general information, numbers, transition signals and discourse markers (firstly, secondly, obviously, furthermore, indeed)

READING

▷ Practising all question types

▷ Skimming (to get a general understanding)

▷ Scanning (looking for specific information)

▷ Developing vocabulary

▷ Summarising

▷ Determining the writer's attitude and opinion

WRITING

▷ Practising all question types

▷ Adjusting style according to purpose

▷ Writing paragraphs, introductions and conclusions

▷ Using conjunctions and referents

▷ Organising information logically within a text

▷ Using examples and evidence to support an argument

SPEAKING

▷ Practising all question types

▷ Practising pronunciation and intonation

▷ Practising fluency

▷ Using and understanding common phrases

▷ Interacting with other speakers

▷ Speaking for an extended time on a particular topic

▷ Discussing that topic

After all of your preparation for the IELTS test, follow these simple suggestions to help ensure the day of the test goes smoothly.

▷ Plan to arrive early (perhaps half an hour) so that if you have unexpected transport problems, or some other delay, you will have enough time to sort them out before the test starts. There is nothing worse than arriving late, upset or flustered. You need all your mental energy for the test!

▷ Don't worry about the parts of the test that are finished, or those yet to come. Concentrate fully on the test you have in front of you.

▷ Use your time carefully. Don't spend too much time on one answer if it means not answering other questions properly. If you finish early use the time to check your answers carefully—you might notice a wrong answer and gain extra marks!

A FINAL WORD

The practice tests in this book are designed to help you understand the nature of the IELTS test. You cannot use your results in these tests to accurately predict your performance in a real IELTS test conducted under test conditions. You can, however, use the practice tests to understand the test format and question types which you are likely to encounter.

Try to relax and do some activities which you enjoy. An occasional break from your studies will give you fresh energy and motivation to continue studying hard! The night before you sit IELTS go to bed early and get plenty of rest!

Good luck!

"I try to listen to at least two English speaking radio or television programs each week. I find this really helps me speed up my comprehension"

UNIT ONE

LISTENING

UNIT **ONE**
THE **LISTENING TEST**

DURATION AND FORMAT

Listening is the first module in the IELTS test, and takes 30 minutes. It consists of four sections of increasing difficulty, and there is a total of 40 questions to answer.

The test is played **ONCE** only. As you listen to each section you will be given time to read the questions, write your answers on the question paper, and then check them. At the end of **Section 4** you will be given 10 minutes to transfer your answers to the Listening Answer Sheet. So, the Listening Test will last **40** minutes in total.

STRUCTURE OF THE TEST

The test consists of four sections.

Sections 1 and 2 are concerned with social situations and needs. These listening passages include:

▷ a conversation between two speakers talking about, for example, opening a bank account or asking directions, and
▷ a monologue about, for example, a tour of a museum or information on part-time English courses.

Sections 3 and 4 are concerned with study-related topics or mini-lectures or talks, with an educational or training focus. These include:

▷ a conversation between up to four people talking about, for example, a school project, and
▷ a monologue, where, for example, a lecturer is talking on a general academic topic.

You will hear a range of English accents and dialects, including Australian, British, North American, New Zealand, Irish and others.

QUESTION TYPES

A variety of questions are used, chosen from the following types:

▷ short answer
▷ multiple choice
▷ matching
▷ classification
▷ summary completion
▷ notes, summary, sentence or gap-fill completion
▷ diagram completion and labelling
▷ table completion
▷ form completion

FACTORS IN THE ASSESSMENT

For each correct answer, one mark is given. The skills on which you will be assessed include:

▷ following instructions and directions
▷ identifying specific information
▷ identifying main ideas
▷ recognising the roles of speakers
▷ understanding and identifying numbers, dates and names
▷ determining when a speaker is expressing a strong opinion, fact or disagreeing politely using intonation
▷ identifying the general meaning of the conversation or monologue

TEST TIPS

👍 Before each listening section is played, always read through the questions quickly and carefully. Identify key words which will give you an idea of what you are about to hear, and what you need to listen for.

👍 Note what questions you must answer: filling in numbers, finding the speaker's opinion or choosing the right description. You will then be able to make the most of what you hear because you will know what to listen for.

👍 If you miss a question move on so that you can maximise the number of correct answers you get for the remaining questions.

UNIT **ONE** THE LISTENING TEST

→ **IDENTIFY YOUR STRENGTHS AND WEAKNESSES**

After completing each practice test consider the following statements and tick any that apply to you.

☐	I have never practised such questions before	**F**
☐	I do not make good use of preview or review time	**T**
☐	I cannot listen and read the questions at the same time	**T**
☐	I do not understand what the question is asking me to do	**T**
☐	I do not understand what I hear	**U**

Using the letter next to each box you have ticked above, refer to page 13-15 for an explanation of how you can improve in these areas.

LISTENING TEST ANSWER SHEET

 You may **photocopy or reproduce** this page.

→ **TRANSFER** your answers from the Listening question pages to this Answer Sheet at the end of the Listening Tests. Use one Answer Sheet for each Practice Listening Test.

1	21
2	22
3	23
4	24
5	25
6	26
7	27
8	28
9	29
10	30
11	31
12	32
13	33
14	34
15	35
16	36
17	37
18	38
19	39
20	40

Listening TOTAL

QUESTIONS **1–8**

LISTEN to the conversation between a student, Angela Tung, and Bob Wills, who is the student adviser at a language school. Complete the form. Write **no more than three words or a number,** for each answer.

TAMWORTH ENGLISH SCHOOL

REQUEST FOR **SPECIAL LEAVE**

Name	*Angela Tung*
Student number	*H5712*

Example

Address **1**

Tamworth, 2340

Telephone number

Course **2**

Teacher's name **3**

Student visa
expiry date **4**

I wish to request
leave in term **5**

Dates of leave **6**   to **7**

Number of working
days missed **8**

QUESTIONS **9–12**

→ **CIRCLE** the appropriate letter **A–D**.

9 **Why does Angela want to take leave?**

A   to visit her aunt and uncle
B   to see the National Gallery
C   to see the Southern Highlands
D   to study more writing

10 **Where is Angela going?**

A   Tamworth
B   Brisbane
C   Armidale
D   Sydney

11 **Who is going with Angela?**

A   her uncle
B   her mother
C   her aunt
D   her father

12 **When will Angela go home to her own country?**

A   in five years
B   in twelve months
C   in two months
D   when her mother goes home

QUESTIONS 13–18

→ **COMPLETE** the calendar while you listen to the CD. Use words from the box. There are more words in the box than you need. Some words may be used more than once.

cleaner	garbage	filters	stove
dry cleaner	charity	gardener	paper
lift	library	electricity	water

Sunday	Monday	Tuesday	Wednesday	Thursday	Friday	Saturday
MAY		**16** _____			**13** _____	
17	18	19	20	21	22	23
	17 _____				**14** _____	
24	25	26	27	28	29	30
18 _____	JUNE				**15** _____	
31	1	2	3	4	5	6

QUESTIONS **19–24**

→ **SELECT** the appropriate letter **A–D**.

19 **Where has Martha gone?**

A   London
B   Sydney
C   New York
D   Paris

20 **Why is Martha away from home?**

A   she's visiting friends
B   she's at a conference
C   she's on business
D   she's setting up a business

21 **Who will Martha meet while she's away?**

A   an old school friend
B   a friend of her mother
C   an old university friend
D   an old teacher

22 **What has Martha left for John?**

A   a letter
B   a meal
C   a book
D   a bill

23 **Who does Martha want John to telephone?**

A   the optometrist
B   the telephone company
C   the doctor
D   the dentist

24 **What is the code for Martha's alarm system?**

A   enter 2190
B   2190 enter
C   9120 enter
D   enter 9120

QUESTIONS **25–29**

→ **COMPLETE** the table below. Write **no more than three words, or a number,** for each answer.

Language School

ENROLMENT FORM

Name of applicant	*Vijay Paresh*
Telephone number	*909 2467*

Example

Language to be learned	25	
Location of class	26	
Time of class	27	
Name of class	28	
Date of commencement of class	29	

QUESTIONS **30–32**

SELECT the appropriate letters **A–D**.

30 Anne is

A Vijay's friend
B Denise's friend
C Vijay's boss
D Denise's boss.

31 When Anne speaks she

A congratulates Denise
B ignores Denise
C criticises Denise
D praises Denise.

32 When Denise replies she

A laughs at Anne
B sympathises with Anne
C argues with Anne
D apologises to Anne.

QUESTIONS **33–36**

→ **LISTEN** to the directions and match the places in questions 33-36 to the appropriate letter **A-H** on the plan.

33 **Reception area, admissions**

_____

34 **Fees office**

_____

35 **Book and stationery supply**

_____

36 **Travel agency**

_____

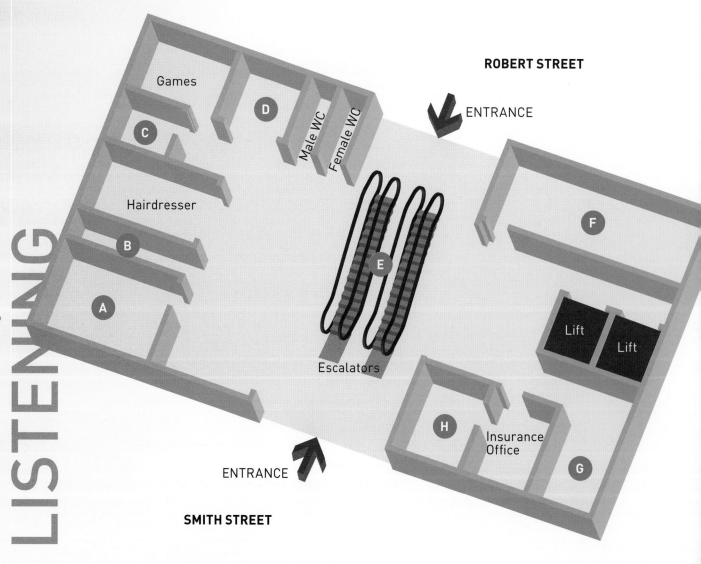

PREPARE FOR IELTS: General Training   UTS:INSEARCH

LISTENING

QUESTIONS **37–38**

→ **LOOK** at **questions** 37-38 below and study the grid. **Tick** all the relevant boxes in each column.

City	**37** Cities with old-structure problems	**38** Cities with good public transport
Los Angeles		
London		
Bangkok		
Hong Kong		
New York		
Taipei		
Houston		
Sydney		
Paris		
Tokyo		
Dallas		

QUESTIONS **39–40**

→ **WRITE no more than three words** to complete these sentences.

39 **The public transport available in Houston is** _____

40 **Vehicles carrying more than one passenger can use** _____

QUESTIONS **1–4**

→ **LISTEN** to the conversation between two people in a shop which sells electronic goods.

Put a **circle** around the letter of the item they choose.

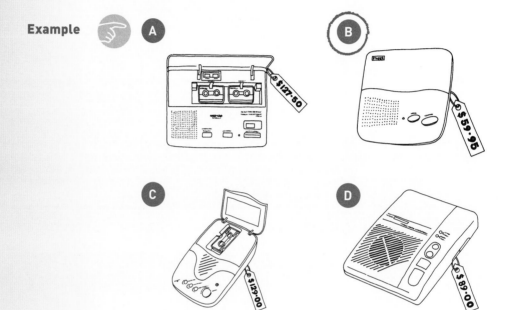

Example 👉 Ⓐ   Ⓑ

Ⓒ   Ⓓ

1

A

B

C

D

2

A

B

C

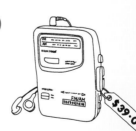

D

3
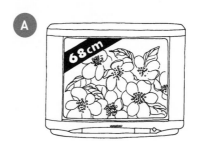

4
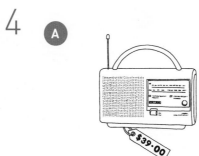

PREPARE FOR IELTS: General Training   UTS:INSEARCH

LISTENING

QUESTIONS **5–10**
WRITE no more than three words for each answer.

→

5 Where will Mary go now?

_____

6 Who is waiting for Tom?

_____

7 What time does Mary expect to come home?

_____

8 Where is Mary's office?

_____

9 What TV program does Tom plan to watch tonight?

_____

10 Where does Tom have to go tomorrow?

_____

QUESTIONS **11–17**

→ **COMPLETE** the Request to Terminate or Transfer Form.

Language School

REQUEST TO
TERMINATE OR **TRANSFER**
CLASSES

Message for   **11** _____

                                      Student Affairs

Student's
family name   **12** _____

Student's
first name   **13** _____

Student number   **14** _____

Teacher's name   **15** _____

Student's address   **16** _____

Telephone   **17** _____

QUESTIONS **18–22**
SELECT the appropriate letter **A–D**.

18 **May wants to change classes because**

A   she doesn't like her teacher
B   too many students share the same language
C   she can't understand the work
D   the class is too large

19 **In the evening class most students' first language is**

A   English
B   Italian
C   Spanish
D   Japanese

20 **There is room in the new class because two students**

A   went home
B   dropped the course
C   transferred
D   graduated

21 **May prefers the evening class because it is**

A   in the same room
B   in the room next door
C   in the same building
D   in the building next door

22 **May wants Mrs Brooks to leave a message at**

A   the library
B   her work
C   her friend's house
D   her home

QUESTIONS **23–27**

→ **COMPLETE** the table showing the students' opinions. Choose your answers from the box below.
There are more words than spaces so you will not use all the words.
You may use any of the words more than once.

INSTRUMENT	STYLE OF MUSIC
guitar	ballet music
violin	rap
pipa	classical
organ	heavy metal
flute	opera
bouzouki	jazz
piano	rock
drums	be-bop
harp	country

	STUDENT	FAVOURITE INSTRUMENT	FAVOURITE STYLE OF MUSIC
Example	Greg	*drums*	*classical*
23	Alexandria		
24	Katja		
25	Rachel		
26	Harry		
27	Emiko		

QUESTIONS **28–31**

→ **WRITE no more than three words** to complete the sentences.

28 Stimulating music speeds up our

_____

29 Calming music reduces our

_____

30 _____

music has very predictable rhythms.

31 Research may show if people of different _____

_____ perceive music differently.

SECTION **FOUR** QUESTIONS **32–40**

QUESTIONS **32–36**

→ **USING no more than three words**, answer the following questions.

32 Who should take charge of the patient's health?

____

33 What, in the speaker's opinion, is the single greatest threat to health?

____

34 Which group in the study was most at risk of early death?

____

35 Which environmental hazard does the speaker find most underrated?

____

36 What will be improved by an education campaign?

____

QUESTIONS **37–40**

→ **WRITE no more than three words** to complete the sentences.

37 Statistics quoted show that _____ would prevent many illnesses.

38 Exercise should be _____ , so find someone to join you in your activity.

39 One important way of preventing sports injury is by adequate

_____

40 Injuries can also be reduced by using _____

_____ techniques.

QUESTIONS **1–5**

→ **LISTEN** to the conversation between the manager of the Student Hostel and a student.
Tick (✔) if the information is correct, or write in the changes.

Student Hostel

CHARGES FOR MEALS

Example	**Breakfast**	$2.00	*$2.50*
	Lunch	$3.00	✔
	Dinner	$3.00	**1** _____
	Three-Meal Plan	$48.00 per week	**2** _____
	Two-Meal Plan	$36.00 per week	**3** _____

MEAL **TIMES**

Breakfast	7:00 – 9:30am	**4** _____
Lunch	noon – 2:00pm	
Dinner	6:00 – 7:30pm	**5** _____

QUESTIONS **6–8**

→ **LISTEN** to the conversation and match the places in questions 6-8 to the appropriate letters **A-F** on the map.

Example   Fees Office   *B*

6   Student Lounge

7   Key Room

8   Box Room

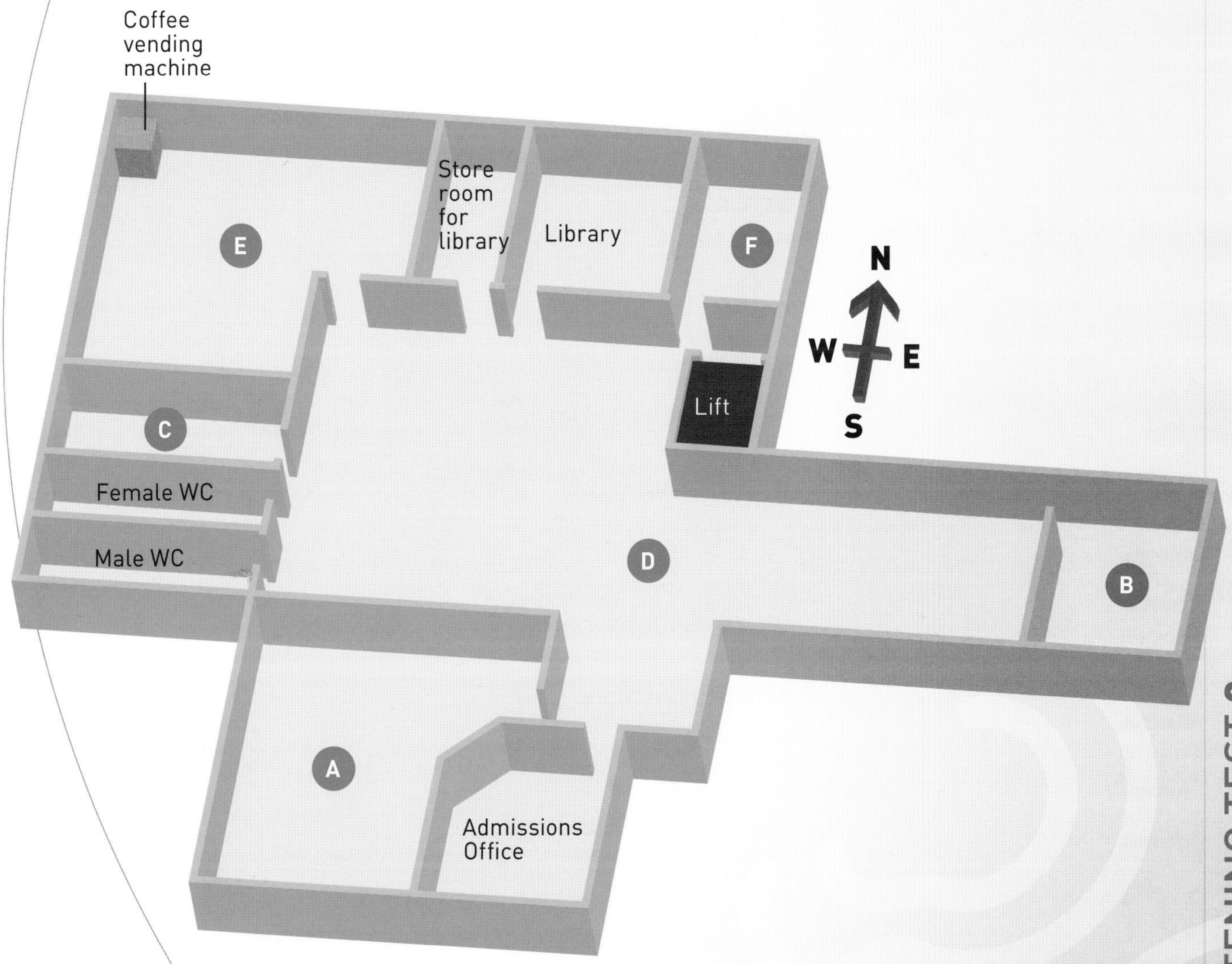

Coffee vending machine

Store room for library

Library

E

F

Lift

N

W   E

S

C

Female WC

Male WC

D

B

A

Admissions Office

QUESTIONS **9–16**

→ **LISTEN** while a teacher tells you how to complete this note. Write **no more than three words or a number** for each answer.

Australian High School

SCHOOL EXCURSION
PERMISSION NOTE

Class   **Example**   *3A*

School
excursion to   **9** _____

on   **10** _____
                          day   date

Bus will depart from   **11** _____   at   **12** _____

Bus will return to   **13** _____   at   **14** _____

Students must bring   **15** _____

Clothing students
will need   **16** _____

**Signature of Guardian/
Group Leader**   _____

→ QUESTIONS **17–19**
WRITE no more than three words or a number for each answer.

17 When will the bus get to the Blue Mountains?

_____

18 What special equipment is on the bus?

_____

19 What other class is going on the excursion?

_____

QUESTIONS **20–22**

→ **COMPLETE** the table which shows when visitors may go to the different parts of the hospital.

	Intensive Care	Maternity	Surgical	Emergency
Permitted visiting hours	☞ *6am – midnight*	**20**	**21**	**22**

QUESTIONS **23–25**

→ **COMPLETE** the table showing who is allowed to visit, and the number of visitors permitted.

A	=	**A**dults may visit
E	=	**E**veryone may visit
I	=	**I**mmediate family only

	Intensive Care	Maternity	Surgical	Emergency
Visitors permitted	☞ *I 2*	**23**	**24**	**25**

QUESTIONS **26–27**

→ **CIRCLE two** letters.

Example

On Monday Andrew will visit these wards

- (A) male surgical
- (B) female surgical
- C children's surgical
- D male geriatric
- E female geriatric
- F infectious diseases.

26 **On Tuesday Andrew will be with**

- A Dr Chang
- B Dr Thomas
- C Dr Gray
- D Dr Robertson
- E Dr Shay
- F Dr Kominski.

27 **On Thursday and Friday Andrew will visit**

- A the nursery
- B the hospital gymnasium
- C the administration office
- D the school room
- E the teenage ward
- F the children's ward.

QUESTIONS **28–30**

→ **WRITE no more than three words or a number** for each answer.

28 **What time on Wednesday morning will Andrew be in lectures?**

_____

29 **How many first-year students are there?**

_____

30 **What job does Andrew's father do?**

_____

QUESTIONS **31–37**

→ **WRITE no more than three words** to complete these sentences.

31 Samuel Wells _____
before Scholastic House opened in 1903.

32 There were _____
original students.

33 Scholastic House became _____
in 1963.

34 One of these students became a prominent

_____

35 Scholastic House experienced difficulties during

_____

36 The college has a tradition of learning and

_____

37 Since 1927, controversial _____
have been discussed.

QUESTIONS **38–40**
→ **CIRCLE** the appropriate letter **A–D**.

38 **The college discusses controversial
issues because it**

A informs the debate
B reduces tension
C encourages argument
D brings positive publicity

39 **The principal believes that**

A science is less advanced than medicine
B philosophy is more useful than science
C science is ahead of philosophy
D science is more useful than philosophy

40 **The principal urges the students to**

A accept what they are told
B ask questions at all times
C think only about their studies
D think where progress will lead them

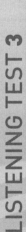

LISTENING TEST 4

QUESTIONS **1–8**

→ **LISTEN** to the conversation and complete the table. Write **C** for Cookery, **S** for Sports and **T** for Travel.

NAME OF AUTHOR	C = Cookery S = Sports T = Travel
Peter Adams	👉 *S T*
Stephen Bau	①
Pam Campbell	②
C. Kezik	*S*
Ari Hussein	③
Sally Innes	*S*
Meg Jorgensen	④
Bruno Murray	⑤
Ruby Lee	⑥
Jim Wells	⑦
Helen Yeung	⑧

LISTENING

→ **LOOK** at this invitation. Tick (✔) if the information is correct **or** write in the changes.

Invitation
§

to a Welcoming Lunch *dance party*

at Blackwell House 　　　　　　✔

on Friday June 15 at 8:00 pm. 　　**9**

The party will end at 10:00 pm. 　**10**

Free transport to the student hostel is available, leaving Blackwell House at 10:30. 　**11**

Other students may attend. 　　**12**

Please bring your student identification card. 　**13**

Please reply by Tuesday, if you can come. 　**14**

→ **COMPLETE** the sentences below. Write **no more than three words** for each answer.

15　There is new road work on

_____

16　Do not use Blackwell Street because workmen are

_____

17　When you pass the roundabout, go along Brown Crescent into

_____

18　It's wise to use the

_____

QUESTIONS **19–23**

→ **LABEL** the parts of the lawn sprinkler, which is used to water grass and gardens. Choose words from the box below. There are more words in the box than you will need.
Write the appropriate words on the diagram.

holes	base	crank
spray tube	handle	gears
hinge	hose pipe	water wheel
guide	chain guard	pulley

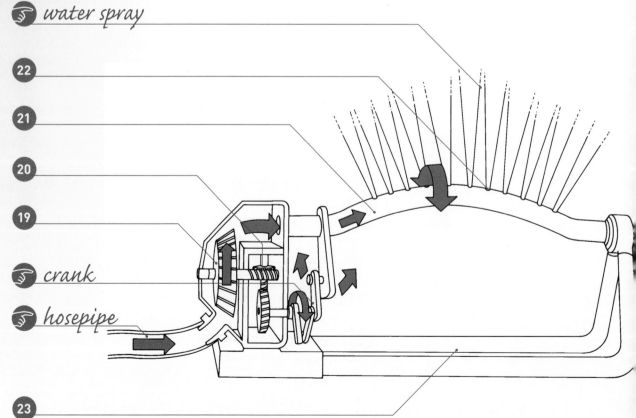

water spray

22

21

20

19

crank

hosepipe

23

LISTENING

QUESTIONS **24–29**
→ **CIRCLE** the appropriate letter **A-D**.

24 **The last examinations will be held on**

A November 26
B November 29
C December 2
D December 4

25 **Scott is going to the United States**

A to study
B to teach
C to travel
D to visit friends

26 **The general science course in the United States is**

A similar
B simple
C difficult
D different

27 **Linda has had an extension to**

A complete her assignment
B do more research
C study
D go on holiday

28 **Communications and English will be examined on**

A December 1 morning
B December 2 morning
C December 1 afternoon
D December 2 afternoon

29 **Mark finds teaching this class**

A boring
B tiring
C depressing
D interesting

QUESTIONS **30–40**

 COMPLETE the summary on the opposite page. Use words from the box. There are more words in the box than you need. Some words may be used more than once.

rest	relaxed	angry	warm
stress	work	hunger	45 degrees
chew	exhaustion	desk	40 degrees
noise	tense	study	crowded
speak	smoky	relaxation	long-term
tired	exercise	raised	

The most usual cause of headaches is

30 _____.

Headaches can also come as a result of excessive

31 _____.

Some people say they get a headache when they

32 _____. This is probably because

they get very 33 _____.

It may also be because they are working in poor light

which makes them very 34 _____.

It is helpful if your reading material is on a bookrest at

35 _____ to the desk. It is also

important to be 36 _____ in bed.

You may even get a headache because you

37 _____ too hard.

The best advice is to try to eat regular meals, get enough

38 _____ and avoid

39 _____ places. These places

can also do you serious 40 _____

damage.

QUESTIONS **1–2**

→ **LISTEN** to the conversation between Megan and Ken about how they will spend the evening. Circle the appropriate letter.

Example

What is Thomas's new home phone number?

A   9731 4322
B   9813 4562
C   9452 3456
D   9340 2367

1   **What will Ken and Megan do this evening?**

2   **Where is Entertainment City?**

PREPARE FOR IELTS: General Training   UTS:INSEARCH

LISTENING

QUESTIONS **3–7**

3 **When will Ken leave?**

A now
B in ten minutes' time
C at 10 o'clock
D in 30 minutes

4 **How will Megan travel to Entertainment City?**

 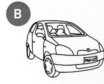 

5 **How many people will they meet there?**

A none
B three
C two
D a group

6 **How much will the evening cost?**

A nothing
B just the fares
C less than $40.00
D more than $40.00

7 **What time does Megan plan to come home?**

A before midnight
B after midnight
C on the last bus
D on the last train

QUESTIONS **8–9**

→ **WRITE one number** for each answer.

Which telephone button will Ken press:

Example **if he wishes to order a cab now?**

_1_

8 **if he wishes to order a cab for later?**

_____

9 **if he has lost something in a cab?**

_____

QUESTIONS **10–15**

→ **COMPLETE** the notes below. Write **no more than three words or a number** for each answer in the spaces provided.

The plane will leave Gatwick Airport at

10_____ in the morning.

The transport from Athens Airport will be by

11_____. The hotel is booked for

12_____ nights. During our stay,

the group will visit the National Archaeological Museum

in the morning. Group members will then have free time

on **13**_____ evening. The group

will see the Greek Islands and will travel by

14_____.

Traditional **15**_____ will be part of

the package.

QUESTIONS **16–18**

CIRCLE two letters

16 **The organiser would like to thank**

A the Greek government
B the travel agent
C British Airways
D staff at the British Museum

17 **People should bring to the party**

A photographs
B food
C camera
D drinks

18 **The members of the group share an interest in**

A Greek culture
B studying old societies
C fine food
D travel

QUESTIONS **19–20**

COMPLETE this baggage label. Write **no more than three words** in the spaces provided.

19 _____

20 _____

LISTENING TEST **5** CONTINUED

QUESTIONS **21–26**

→ **WRITE** no more than three words or a number for each answer.

21 When did the Language Learning Centre enter its new building?

_____

22 Which country do most of the students come from now?

_____

23 What were the Indonesians studying at the Language Learning Centre?

_____

24 How long should students stay at the Language Learning Centre?

_____

25 What is the most common class size?

_____

26 Who does Dr Robinson consider to be the best promoters of the Centre?

_____

QUESTIONS **27–31**

→ **COMPLETE** the table showing which activities are available.
Tick (✔) in the column if an activity is available.

	ACTIVITY	ALL STUDENTS	BEGINNERS	ADVANCED STUDENTS
Example ☞	Soccer Club	✔		
27	Non-English language courses			
28	Jazz Club			
29	Drama Society			
30	Choral Group			
31	Special conversation group			

→ **NB.** When transferring your answers to the answer sheet, you should write **ALL** or **BEGINNERS** or **ADVANCED**.

QUESTIONS **32–37**

→ **CIRCLE** the appropriate letter **A–D**

32 Most postgraduate students are studying

- **A** courses that feature vocational training
- **B** full-time courses
- **C** part-time courses
- **D** research-based courses

33 Postgraduate students are advised to

- **A** take as many diverse subjects as possible
- **B** accept an intellectual challenge
- **C** be sure to have a definite goal
- **D** have already completed training

34 The speaker says that where you study

- **A** is of minimal importance
- **B** must be somewhere you like
- **C** must be reasonably priced
- **D** should be based on your course

35 Choosing an institution should be mainly based on

- **A** the quality of the housing for postgraduate students
- **B** the reputation of the department they work in
- **C** the reputation of the organisation they attend
- **D** the quality of the supervision they receive

36 These facilities are the most important to the speaker:

- **A** libraries and laboratories
- **B** computer facilities
- **C** secretarial support
- **D** recreational organisations

37 Postgraduates can avoid feeling alone by

- **A** joining associations of their peers
- **B** developing outside interests
- **C** participating in the outside community
- **D** making friends outside the university

SECTION FOUR CONTINUED

QUESTIONS **38–40**

COMPLETE the sentences below. Write **no more than three words** for each answer.

38 Students should not forget to budget for their

____

39 Students should check all study costs carefully because institutions may

____

40 Postgraduate students cannot get loans from

____

"Learning to scan an article or report for the most important information is essential— especially when you're working to a deadline!"

UNIT **TWO**

READING

DURATION AND FORMAT

Reading is the second part of the IELTS test, and takes 60 minutes. It consists of three or sometimes four reading passages of increasing difficulty, and there is a total of 40 questions to answer. Though you can mark and write on the Question Paper, you must enter your answers on the Reading Answer Sheet, and be aware that no extra time is given for transfering your answers.

STRUCTURE OF THE TEST

The texts for the **three** or sometimes **four** reading passages are based on the kinds of information you would encounter in every day life situations. The passages would be sourced from advertisements (eg. job advertisement or notices), timetables (e.g. train timetable), instructions (e.g. manual on how to operate an iPod), official documents (e.g. passport), menus, newspapers, books and magazines.

Section 1 relates to social situations in an English-speaking context. **Section 2** relates to a training context, while **Section 3** or **4** includes extended prose or articles, using more complex language.

QUESTION TYPES

There is a variety of question types used in the reading, including:

▷ short answer
▷ multiple choice
▷ matching headings or lists
▷ viewpoint questions (consider the viewpoint of the writer —True/False/Not Given or Yes/No/No Information
▷ classification
▷ notes, summary, sentence or gap-fill completion
▷ diagram completion and labelling
▷ table completion
▷ flow-chart completion

FACTORS IN THE ASSESSMENT

For each correct answer, one mark is given. The skills on which you will be assessed include:

▷ identifying and retrieving factual information
▷ understanding the writer's viewpoint
▷ distinguishing between opinion, fact or assumption
▷ understanding the main points of a passage by recognising ways of linking ideas, sentences and paragraphs, e.g. cause and effect language, time sequences, comparison or contrast
▷ locating detailed information

TEST TIPS

👍 You have one hour to answer questions in three sections so divide up your time, carefully. The sections become increasingly difficult so allocate perhaps 15 minutes for the first section, 20 minutes for the second and 25 minutes for the third section.

👍 Start each reading section by finding out what information you are looking for. Read the questions first. You will waste precious time if you try to read and understand everything.

Read the heading. This will give you a good general idea of what the passage is about.

Read through the questions quickly. How many are there? What sort of questions are they (sentence completion, diagram completion etc.)? This will help you focus when you read the text as you will have some ideas of what to look for.

Scan and skim the text. You do not need to understand every detail. This is to get a general understanding of the passage.

Turn back to the questions and begin to work through them, referring back to the passage as you need to and reading the important sections carefully and slowly.

If you cannot answer a question, or it is taking you a long time, leave it and come back to it at the end.

👍 When completing the practice tests, remember to write your answers straight onto the answer sheet. DO NOT write your answers on the question pages because in the real IELTS test all answers must be written on the Answer Sheet.

→ **IDENTIFY** YOUR STRENGTHS AND WEAKNESSES

After each test consider the following statements and tick any that apply to you.

☐	I have never practised such questions before	**F**
☐	I run out of time and do not answer all the questions	**T**
☐	It takes me a long time to read the passages	**T**
☐	I do not understand what the question is asking me to do	**T**
☐	I do not understand the reading passages	**U**

Using the letter next to each box you have ticked above, refer to page 13-15 for an explanation of how you can improve in these areas.

READING TEST ANSWER SHEET

You may **photocopy or reproduce** this page.

→ **USE** one Answer Sheet for each Practice Reading Test.

1		21	
2		22	
3		23	
4		24	
5		25	
6		26	
7		27	
8		28	
9		29	
10		30	
11		31	
12		32	
13		33	
14		34	
15		35	
16		36	
17		37	
18		38	
19		39	
20		40	

Reading TOTAL

READING TEST **1**

→ **ON** the following page is a contents page from a magazine. **Answer questions 1–3** by writing the appropriate page number or numbers where the information appears in the magazine, in **boxes 1–3** on your answer sheet.

Example On what page is the main article in the magazine?

5

1 What page would you turn to for advice about money?

2 On what TWO pages can you read about art?

3 On what page is the new sports stadium discussed?

QUESTION **4**

→ **ANSWER** Question 4 by writing **no more than three words** in box 4 on your answer sheet.

4 How often does this magazine appear?

Why
MAGAZINE

FROM THE EDITOR

In this issue we publish some of the many letters we received on the new Sports Stadium, our cover story last month. Your reactions were certainly mixed! Read our exclusive interview with film star Mike Mikeson and his plans to start a fast-food chain. But there's so much more ... enough to keep you going for the rest of the month.

Until next time,

The Editor

→ **READ** the advertisements for concerts below and answer **questions** **5–10** that follow.

SYDNEY CONSERVATORIUM OF MUSIC

Concerts for January

A   **THE EASTERN YOUTH ORCHESTRA**

Conservatorium High School students play a selection of Mozart concertos.

DATE: Sat. 7th and 14th January, 8:00 pm. $10 and $5

B   **LET'S SING TOGETHER**

An afternoon for the young and the young-at-heart. Led by the Giggles Band, sing children's songs from your childhood and from all over the world.

There will be a special appearance by Willy Wallaby, from the popular children's programme, *Hoppy!*

DATE: Sun. 8th January, 3:00 pm. $5

C   **ONE ROMANTIC EVENING**

Bring someone special with you and listen to some of the greatest love songs as you gaze at the stars together!

DATE: Sat. 28th January, 8:00 pm. $20 and $12

NOTE: *This concert will be held in the Conservatorium Rose Garden, not in the Concert Hall.*

D   **ROCK N' ROLL**

Bop along 'til late to the rock hits of the last 10 years. Bands playing include The Hippies, The Hypers, and The Heroes. If you have a special request, write it down at the ticket counter when you come in.

DATE: Sat. 21st January, 8:00 pm. $10 and $5

E   **FLAMENCO!**

World-famous classical guitarist Rodrigo Paras will play a selection of traditional Spanish Flamenco pieces.

DATE: Sun. 15th and 22nd January, 7:30 pm. $20 and $12

→ **ANSWER** questions **5–10** below by writing the appropriate letter or letters **A-E** in **boxes 5-10** on your answer sheet. Your answer may require more than one letter.

Example At which concert will a television character appear?

B

5 At which concert will young performers play?

6 Which concert will be held outdoors?

7 Which concerts will happen more than once?

8 Which concert will feature only one performer?

9 Which concert is NOT being held at night?

10 At which concert can the audience choose what will be performed?

→ **READ** the information below on treatment for snake bites, then
answer **questions 11–15**.

FIRST AID FOR SNAKE BITES

Snakes are not normally aggressive and tend to bite only when they
are threatened or mishandled. Some snakes, e.g. the carpet snake,
are not poisonous. Others, e.g. the brown snake, tiger snake and
taipan, are very poisonous.

A Prevention
- ✗ leave snakes alone and do not collect snakes
- ✗ do not put your hands in hollow logs, under piles of wood, or in
  rubbish
- ✔ be noisy when walking in the bush
- ✔ look carefully when walking through thick grass
- ✔ use a torch around camps at night

B Symptoms and signs
These do not appear immediately, but from about 15 minutes to
2 hours after the person is bitten. There are often no visible
symptoms or signs. Take seriously any information from the person
concerning:

- ➤ strong emotional reaction
- ➤ headache or double vision
- ➤ drowsiness, giddiness or faintness
- ➤ nausea and/or vomiting and diarrhoea
- ➤ puncture marks about 1 centimetre apart at the site of the bite.
  Bites are usually on the limbs, especially the legs.
- ➤ reddening
- ➤ bruising
- ➤ sweating
- ➤ breathing difficulties

C Management
- ➤ reassure the person
- ➤ apply a pressure immobilisation bandage over the bitten area and
  around the limb
- ➤ seek medical aid urgently

D Snakebite Warnings
- ➤ **never** wash the venom off the skin as this will help
  in later identification
- ➤ **never** cut or squeeze the bitten area
- ➤ **never** try to suck the venom out of the wound

→ **THE** passage "First Aid for Snake Bites" explains what to do in the event of a snake bite.
Read the statements below and choose the section **A-D** to which each statement belongs. Write the appropriate letter in **boxes 11-15** on your answer sheet.

Example   • **never use a tight bandage**

D

11   • **help the person to sit or lie down**

12   • **wear stout shoes, walk socks and jeans (or similar clothing) in areas where snakes could be present**

13   • **pain or tightness in the chest or abdomen**

14   • **do not try to catch the snake**

15   • **swelling of the bitten area**

→ **READ** "Student Accommodation at Northside University" below and answer **questions 16–25** that follow.

STUDENT ACCOMMODATION AT **NORTHSIDE UNIVERSITY**

Situated about 20km from the city centre, **Northside University** is not easy to get to by public transport. However, students have several different alternatives for accommodation on or near the University campus.

Firstly, the University has several residential colleges; Burnside College, Boronia College and Helen Turner College. Each of these colleges provides a single fully furnished room with shared bathroom facilities, and meals. Burnside College is the most expensive, with 2006 fees ranging from $154 - $165 per week. However, each student room is equipped with a private telephone and voice-mailing facilities, and within the next few months college students will have access to E-MAIL, On-Line library, INTERNET and AARNET via a network with the University. Boronia College has similar room facilities but does not offer the same computer access. It also offers only 17 meals per week, compared to Burnside's 21. Fees vary from $147 - $157 per week. Helen Turner College is a college exclusively for women, with similar fees to Boronia College. To attend classes, students have a short walk from the residential colleges to the main University campus.

The University also provides 23 self-contained furnished townhouses. These townhouses have either 3, 4 or 6 bedrooms each and student residents are expected to be studying full-time. Rents in 2000 ranged from $54 per week for a room in a six bedroom flat to $68.50 per week for a room in a three-bedroom house. Students wanting to live in university housing should apply to the university housing officer in August of the previous year, as it is in high demand. Smoking is banned in University housing.

Off campus, there are many flats, town houses and houses for rent in the local area. These can be found by looking in the local newspaper under ACCOMMODATION, or by checking notices pinned up on the boards around the university. There are always students advertising for housemates and you can even add a notice of your own to the board. However, even sharing accommodation with others can be expensive; tenants are usually required to pay a rental bond, rent in advance, and telephone/electricity/gas bills in addition to food bills. Be sure that you know what you will be required to pay before you enter into any written agreement.

QUESTIONS **16–19**

→ **CHOOSE** the appropriate letter **A–C** and write it in **boxes 16-19** on your answer sheet.

16 **The University Residential Colleges provide**

A a place to live and regular classes
B regular classes only
C a place to live only.

17 **Smoking is**

A allowed in University housing
B not allowed in University housing
C allowed only in certain areas in University housing.

18 **University town houses are available for**

A full-time students only
B part-time students only
C all students.

19 **Accommodation in the area surrounding the university is**

A scarce
B plentiful
C scarce and expensive.

QUESTIONS **20–25**

→ **COMPLETE** the following sentences with information from the passage. Write your answers in **boxes 20-25** on your answer sheet.

A student living in a 3-bedroom University town house would pay __20__ per week for a room; in comparison, the cheapest accommodation available at Burnside College is __21__ per week. The fee charged at Burnside College includes __22__ meals per week, but at Boronia College only __23__ meals per week are included in the fee. Helen Turner College has a similar fee structure to __24__ College, but only __25__ may live there.

→ **READ** the passage below and answer **questions 26–40** that follow.

KORMILDA COLLEGE

Section A
Kormilda College is a unique school situated near Darwin in Australia's Northern Territory. For 20 years, to 1989, Kormilda College operated as a government-run, live-in school for high school Aboriginal students. In 1989 it was bought from the Government by two Christian church groups and since then it has expanded enormously, to include a day school as well as boarders (residential students) in Years 8-12. Although 320 pupils of the College's total number are Aboriginal students, drawn mainly from isolated communities across the Northern Territory, Kormilda also has a waiting list of non-Aboriginal students. With a current enrolment of 600, student numbers are expected to grow to 860 by 2005.

Section B
Central to the mission of the school is the encouragement of individual excellence, which has resulted in programs designed especially for the student population. Specialist support programs allow traditional Aboriginal students, who are often second language users, to understand and succeed in the mainstream curriculum. A Gifted and Talented Program, including a special Aboriginal and Torres Strait Islander Tertiary Aspirations program, has been introduced, as has an Adaptive Education Unit. Moreover, in Years 11 and 12, students may choose to follow the standard Northern Territory Courses, or those of the International Baccalaureate (I.B.).

Section C
To provide appropriate pastoral care, as well as a suitable academic structure, three distinct sub-schools have been established.

- **Pre-Secondary:** For Aboriginal and Torres Strait Islander students in Years 8-10 who are of secondary school age but have difficulties reading and writing.

- **Supported Secondary:** For Aboriginal and Torres Strait Islander students who are of secondary school age and operating at secondary school year levels 8-12 who need specific second language literacy and numeracy support.

- **Secondary:** For multi-cultural Years 8-12 students.

Students remain in their sub-schools for classes in the main subject areas of English, Mathematics, Social Education and Science. This arrangement takes into account both diverse levels of literacy and the styles of learning and cultural understandings appropriate to traditional Aboriginal second-language users. In elective subjects chosen by the students—which include Indonesian, Music, Art, Drama, Science for Life, Commerce, Geography, Modern History, Woodwork, Metalwork, Economics and Legal Studies—students mix on the basis of subject interest.

Section D

To aid the development of the Aboriginal Education program, a specialist curriculum Support Unit has been set up. One of its functions is to re-package school courses so that they can be taught in ways that suit the students.

The education program offered to Aboriginal students uses an approach which begins with the students' own experiences and gradually builds bi-cultural understanding. In one course, "Introducing Western European Culture Through Traditional Story-Telling", students are helped to build a common base for approaching the English literature curriculum. Drawing on the oral culture of traditional Aboriginal communities, they are introduced to traditional stories of other cultures, both oral and written. In a foundational Year 10 course, "Theory of Learning", concepts from Aboriginal culture are placed side by side with European concepts so that students can use their own knowledge base to help bridge the cultural divide.

Another project of the Support Unit has been the publication of several books, the most popular, **Kormilda Capers.** The idea for **Kormilda Capers** came about when it became obvious that there was a lack of engaging material for the school's teenage readers. One of the stories in the book, "The Bulman Mob hits the Big Smoke", recounts the adventures of Kormilda pupils on their first visit to Sydney, Canberra and the snow country. Focussing on experiences which have directly affected the lives of students at the College, and on ideas and issues which are of immediate interest to Aboriginal students, **Kormilda Capers** has earned enthusiastic support within and outside the school.

QUESTIONS **26–27**

→ **COMPLETE** the following sentences with **a number or date** from the passage. Write your answers in **boxes 26-27** on your answer sheet.

26 Kormilda College opened as a school in _____

27 At the time of writing there were _____
    non-Aboriginal students at Kormilda College.

QUESTION **28**

→ **FROM the list below**, choose the best heading for **Section B** of the reading passage. Write the appropriate letter **A-D** in **box 28** on your answer sheet.

A   Specialist teaching and teachers at Kormilda College

B   Special Programs at Kormilda College for Aboriginal students

C   The new look Kormilda College

D   Programs at Kormilda College to promote individual excellence

QUESTIONS **29–33**

→ **THE following diagram** shows how Kormilda College is organised. Complete the diagram using information from the text. Use **no more than three words** for each answer. Write your answers in **boxes 29-33** on your answer sheet.

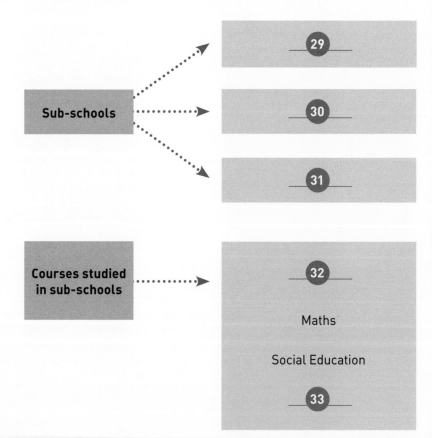

QUESTIONS **34–40**

READ the passage about Kormilda College and look at the statements below. In **boxes 34-40** on your answer sheet write:

TRUE	if the statement is true
FALSE	if the statement is false
NOT GIVEN	if the information is not given in the passage

34 Kormilda College educates both Aboriginal and non-Aboriginal students.

35 Some students travel from Arnhem Land to attend Kormilda College.

36 Students must study both the International Baccalaureate and Northern Territory courses.

37 The Pre-Secondary School attracts the best teachers.

38 The specialist curriculum Support Unit adapts school courses so the students can approach them more easily.

39 There are no oral traditional stories in Western communities.

40 The school helps the students make connections between Aboriginal and non-Aboriginal cultures.

READING TEST **2**

QUESTIONS **1–6**

 THERE are five advertisements A–E on the next page.

Answer **questions 1–6** below by writing the letters of the appropriate advertisements in **boxes 1-6** on your answer sheet.

1   Which advertisement is not for a restaurant?

2   Which **two** advertisements offer facilities for parties?

3   Which restaurant states that it serves breakfast?

4   Which restaurant will give you an extra serving if you present the coupon?

5   Which restaurant does not offer a takeaway service?

6   Which restaurant will bring the food you order to your house?

A

IT'S YOUR CHOICE
Buy a Burger, get the same one FREE!
You are invited to enjoy a special treat at Jaspar's Macquarie Plaza.
Simply present this coupon with your next order and when you purchase the burger of your choice it will be our pleasure to give you another burger of the same variety absolutely FREE!
Valid only at Macquarie and ONE voucher per customer per day.

JASPAR'S

MACQUARIE PLAZA NORTH RICHMOND

Expires 9th May, 2007. Cannot be used with any other Jaspar's offer.

Eat in or Takeaway
LEVEL 3, NEXT TO THE CINEMA COMPLEX

B

T R E L L I N I S
R E S T A U R A N T

Fine Italian Food
BYO Eat In ❖ Takeaway
OPEN Lunch ❖ Dinner

Now: Better Menu – Food – Service
Superb Winter Dishes and Dessert

Perfect for Parties
Separate party rooms and choice of set menu available for 10-80 people and value for $$$

Ph 9271 8600 | 12 Oxford St. EPPING
Opp. PO. Ample parking

C

BYO
No Corkage
and licensed

9693 2258
9693 2260

INDIAN *Flavour*

DINNER **7** NIGHTS

- 10% discount on takeaways
- Free home delivery *(local areas only)*
- Banquet—only $16.50 per person
- Separate party room *(up to 90 people)*

63–65 John Street, RYDE

D

writers' cafe

Dante Trattoria, Shop 4, Spring Centre, Soldier's Road, Neutral Bay

PHONE	9953 1212
OPEN	8am-midnight
CUISINE	Italian influence, menu changes every four months. Breakfast includes toast, pancakes, smoked salmon, scrambled eggs, gourmet sausages and fruit; light meals and lunch menu includes pasta, salad, crepes, seafood, soups, focaccia, burgers and desserts.
PRICES	Breakfast $4.50 - $8.90 Lunch $6.90 - $13.90
ATMOSPHERE	Relaxed and quiet. Patrons can dine inside or out.
CREDIT CARDS	Yes

E

vegetarian
COOKING CLASSES

Are you looking for some **healthy alternatives** to your menu?

Join our creative and nutritious three-week program conducted by qualified professionals, including delicious tastings and demonstrations.

Starting Wednesday May 10 at 7.15 pm.

Centre for Health Management

SYDNEY DAY HOSPITAL
BOOK NOW 9748 9696

THE following text is a series of general instructions for using a microwave oven.
Part of each instruction is underlined. Answer **questions 7–12** on your answer sheet write:

E	if the underlined section gives an **EXAMPLE** of the instruction
R	if the underlined section gives a **REASON** for the instruction
CP	if the underlined section is a **CORRECT PROCEDURE.**

QUESTIONS **7–12**

GENERAL INSTRUCTIONS
FOR THE USE OF
YOUR **MICROWAVE**

Example Do not boil eggs in their shell (unless otherwise stated).
<u>Pressure will build up and the eggs will explode.</u>

7 Whilst heating liquids which contain air (e.g. milk or milk-based fluids), stir several times during heating <u>to avoid spillage of the liquid from the container.</u>

8 <u>Potatoes, apples, egg yolks, whole squash and sausages are all foods with non-porous skins.</u> This type of food must be pierced before cooking, to prevent bursting.

9 Do not dry clothes or other materials in the oven. <u>They may catch on fire.</u>

10 Do not cook food directly on glass oven tray unless indicated in recipes. <u>Food should be placed in a suitable cooking utensil.</u>

11 Do not hit control panel. <u>Damage to controls may occur.</u>

12 <u>Clean the oven, the door and the seals with water and a mild detergent at regular intervals.</u> Never use an abrasive cleaner that may scratch the surfaces around the door.

→ **READ** the "Guided Walks and Nature Activities" information below, and answer **Questions 13-18**.

Ku-ring-gai Chase National Park

GUIDED WALKS AND NATURE ACTIVITIES

SUNDAY MAY 7   *EASY*
Early Morning Stroll in Upper Lane Cove Valley

Meet at 7.30 am at the end of Day Rd, Cheltenham while the bush is alive with birdsong.

Round trip: 4 hours

FRIDAY MAY 12   *MEDIUM*
Possum Prowl

Meet 7.30 pm at Seaforth Oval carpark. Enjoy the peace of the bush at night. Lovely water views. Bring flashlight and wear non-slip shoes as some rock clambering involved. Coffee and biscuits supplied.

Duration: 2 hours

SUNDAY JUNE 4   *HARD*
Bairne / Basin Track

Meet 9.30 am Track #8, West Head Road. Magnificent Pittwater views. Visit Beechwood cottage. Bring lunch and drink. Some steep sections. Reasonable fitness required.

Duration: approx. 6 hours.

FRIDAY JUNE 16   *EASY*
Poetry around a mid-winter campfire

Meet 7.00 pm Kalkaari Visitor Centre. Share your favourite poem or one of your own with a group around a gently crackling fire. Billy tea and damper to follow. Dress up warmly. Bring a mug and a rug (or a chair).
Cost $4.00 per person.

Duration: 2.5 hours

SUNDAY JUNE 25   *EASY*
Morning Walk at Mitchell Park

Meet 8.30 am entrance to Mitchell Park, Mitchell Park Rd, Cattai for a pleasant walk wandering through rainforest, river flats and dry forest to swampland. Binoculars a must to bring, as many birds live here. Finish with morning tea.

Duration: 3 hours.

GRADING

EASY	suitable for ALL fitness levels
MEDIUM	for those who PERIODICALLY exercise
HARD	only if you REGULARLY exercise

QUESTIONS **13–18**

BELOW is a chart containing some of the Ku-ring-gai Chase National Park Nature Activities. Fill in the blanks using information from the brochure "Guided Walks and Nature Activities". Write **no more than three words** in **boxes 13-18** on your answer sheet.

ACTIVITY	What to bring/wear	What is supplied	Chief Attraction
Early Morning Stroll			_____ 13 _____
Morning Walk	_____ 14 _____		varied landscape, birds
Poetry	warm clothes, mug, rug/chair, poem flashlight	_____ 15 _____	
_____ 16 _____	_____ 17 _____	coffee, biscuits	peace, _____ 18 _____

→ **BELOW** are the course descriptions for five courses offered by a local community college. Read the descriptions and answer **questions 19–29**.

COMMUNITY COLLEGE COURSES

COURSE A

If you have no previous experience with computers, or you have some gaps in your knowledge of the basics, then this is an appropriate course for you. This course will give you a thorough grounding in the fundamental concepts of computing common to all computers. It is a practical "hands on" course that looks at how a computer operates and how the programs work. Using three of the most widely used programs in business, you will learn the basics of word processing, spreadsheets and databases. By the completion of the course you will be productive at a basic level and competent to progress to the elementary level of any of the specialised programs. No previous computer skills assumed.

Duration:	2 days	
Fee:	$279	
25045	Wed/Thurs 12, 13 April	9.15 am–5.15 pm
25006	Tues/Wed 30, 31 May	9.15 am–5.15 pm

COURSE B

In dealing with your customers you are in a position of great importance. Your abilities directly influence the company's bottom line. This course will look at ways to revitalise the customer contact skills you already have and add many more. Learn ways to improve your communication with customers, at all levels, techniques to use with difficult customers, how to confidently handle complaints and keep your cool in stressful situations. Most importantly, you will learn to build goodwill and trust with your customers. Course notes, lunch and refreshments provided.

Tutor:	Joshua Smith	
Fee:	$145	
25026	Sat 20 May	9.00 am–4.00 pm

PREPARE FOR IELTS: General Training   UTS:INSEARCH

READING

COURSE C

Everything you need to know before purchasing or starting a coffee shop, tearooms or small restaurant. A useful course for all aspiring owners, managers and employees of these small businesses to assist them in ensuring they don't make expensive mistakes and that their customers return again and again ... Bring lunch. Notes and manual available (if required) for $25 from Tutor.

Tutor:	Sarah Bridge	
Fee:	$55 (no concession)	
25252	Sat 6 May	10.00 am–3.00 pm

COURSE D

This course covers three areas of business communication:
- Interpersonal Communication
- Telephone Skills
- Business Writing Skills

Learning Outcomes

At the end of the course, participants will be able to effectively: plan and write workplace documents in plain English; gather, record and convey information using the telephone and in a face-to-face situation and interact with clients within and external to the workplace about routine matters using the telephone and face-to-face contact. An excellent course for those entering or returning to the workforce. A Statement of Competency is issued if the assessment requirements are successfully completed.

Tutor:	Douglass McDougall	
Fee:	$135	
25021	Wed 3 May-21 June	7.00–9.00 pm

COURSE E

Are you hating work, wanting a different job, needing a change or wanting a promotion? Come along to a new two-day program for women. We will explore your work goals and what holds you back; your fears in a work environment and how you handle them; your image and what it says to others and your communication style and what it says. You will develop more confidence to make changes, get clearer about what you want and have the courage to act. It is a relaxed, informative and fun workshop with lots of practical tips!

Tutor:	Sophie Bradley	
Fee	$199	
25036	Sun 18, 25 June	9.30 am–4.30 pm

→ QUESTIONS **19–23**

CHOOSE the title which best fits each course and write the number I to IX in **boxes 19-23** on your answer sheet. Note: there are more titles than you will need.

I	Managing Expansion In Your Restaurant
II	Making Career Changes For Women
III	Effective Workplace Communication
IV	Exceptional Customer Service
V	Advanced Computing Skills
VI	Communicating Effectively
VII	Introductory Computer Skills
VIII	Restaurant Management For Non-managers
IX	Business Writing Course

Course **A**: _____ 19 _____

Course **B**: _____ 20 _____

Course **C**: _____ 21 _____

Course **D**: _____ 22 _____

Course **E**: _____ 23 _____

QUESTIONS **24–28**

FROM the information about the courses, answer Questions 24–28 by writing the appropriate letter or letters **A–E** in **boxes 24–28** on your answer sheet.

24 Which course is not specifically related to people's jobs?

25 In which course are men not invited to participate?

26 Which **two** courses have course notes to go with them?

27 Which course will deal with writing skills?

28 Which course is on at night?

QUESTION **29**

THREE of the courses specifically cover the same subject. Choose the subject from the list below and write its name in **box 29** on your answer sheet.

Writing skills

Computers

Communication

Finance

Work goals

Management

→ **THE** reading passage below describes some of the great inventions.
From the information given, answer **questions 30–40.**

GREAT **INVENTIONS**

There are some things we use every day. Can you imagine a world
without zippers to fasten clothing? Have you ever wondered about
the layout of the keyboard of a typewriter, which we see every day on
the computer? These are just two of the many inventions which have
made our lives easier. Maybe that's why we don't think about them
very much!

THE ZIPPER

Whatever did we do before the invention of the zipper?

In 1893 the world's first zipper was produced in Chicago. Although
the inventor claimed that it was a reliable fastening for clothing, this
was not the case. The Chicago zipper sprang open without warning,
or jammed shut, and it swiftly lost popularity. Twenty years later a
Swedish-born engineer called Sundback solved the problem. He
attached tiny cups to the backs of the interlocking teeth, and this
meant that the teeth could be enmeshed more firmly and reliably.

At first zippers were made of metal. They were heavy, and if they got
stuck it was difficult to free them. Then came nylon zippers which
were lighter and easier to use, and had smaller teeth. The fashion
industry liked the new zippers far better because they did not distort
the line of the garment or weigh down light fabrics. They were also
easier for the machinists to fit into the garment.

Meanwhile a new fastening agent made its appearance at the end of
the twentieth century: velcro. Velcro is another product made from
nylon. Nylon is a very tough synthetic fibre first developed in the
1930s, and bearing a name to remind the hearer of the two places
where it was developed: NY for New York and LON for London.
Velcro is made with very small nylon hooks on one side of the
fastening which catch tiny looped whiskers on the other side of the
fastening. It is strong and durable.

Velcro is used on clothing, luggage and footwear. It is quick and easy
to fasten and unfasten, and has taken a large part of the zipper's
share of the market. It is also used in ways a zipper cannot be
used—for instance as an easily changed fastening on plaster casts,
and to hold furnishing fabrics in position.

THE TYPEWRITER AND THE KEYBOARD

The keyboard of the modern typewriter is laid out in a most odd fashion. Why would anyone place the letters on the left side of the top row of the keyboard in the order Q W E R T Y? The answer is simple: to slow the typist down. But first, let's consider the history of the typewriter itself.

In the 1860's a newspaper editor called Christopher Sholes lived in Milwaukee, USA. Sholes invented the first of the modern typewriters, although there had been patents for typewriter-like machines as early as 1714, when Queen Anne of England granted a patent to a man called Henry Mill for a machine which would make marks on paper "so neat and exact as not to be distinguished from print". In 1829, across the Atlantic in Detroit USA, William Austin Burt took out a patent on a typewriter-like machine, four years before the French inventor Xavier Projean produced his machine designed to record words at a speed comparable to someone writing with a pen.

So the typewriter was not a new idea, although there had not been a successful realisation of the idea before Christopher Sholes's machine. His typewriter became very popular, and soon people learned to type very quickly—so quickly, in fact, that the keys became tangled. On manual typewriters the characters were set on the end of bars which rose to strike the paper when the key was pressed. In the first models, the keys were set alphabetically. When a quick typist tapped out a word like federal, it was very likely the adjacent e and d keys would become entangled.

Sholes therefore set about finding ways to slow the typist down. He looked for the letters which were most often used in English, and then placed them far away from each other. For instance, q and u, which are almost always used together in English, are separated by five intervening letters. The plan worked, and the typist was slowed down a little.

When computers came into use in the latter part of the twentieth century it was suggested that the keyboard should be rationalised. After all, there was no longer any need to avoid clashing manual typewriter keys. One new board included keys which produced letters which frequently occur together in English, like ing and th and ed, so the word thing would take two strokes to write instead of five. Although this made perfect sense, people found it very hard to learn to use a new keyboard, and the idea was dropped. It is unlikely that the keyboard will ever be changed: as we approach the twenty-first century the voice-activated computer, already in an advanced state of development, is becoming more and more accessible. It is very likely that we will soon have machines which take dictation as we speak to them, and the keyboard will be used for corrections.

QUESTIONS **30–35**

→ **FROM** the information in the reading passage, classify the following events as occurring:

A before the nineteenth century

B during the nineteenth century

C in the first half of the twentieth century

or D at the end of the twentieth century

→ **ANSWER questions 30-35** by writing the appropriate letters **A–D** on your answer sheet.

30 **Sundback's zipper**

31 **the development of nylon**

32 **the development of velcro**

33 **the development of the first typewriter-like machine**

34 **the first appearance of Sholes's typewriter**

35 **the development of the voice-activated computer**

QUESTIONS **36-40**

READ the passage about great inventions and look at the statements below. In **boxes 36-40** on your answer sheet write

TRUE	if the statement is true
FALSE	if the statement is false
NOT GIVEN	if the information is not given in the passage

36   The first zipper was successful as a fastener.

37   Nylon was used a lot during the Second World War, 1939–1945.

38   The first typewriter's keyboard was different to the modern keyboard.

39   The keys of Sholes's first machine were likely to jam.

40   New computers will use the rationalised keyboard.

→ **USE** information in the description below to answer **Questions 1 to 3**. Write your answer in **boxes 1-3** on your answer sheet.

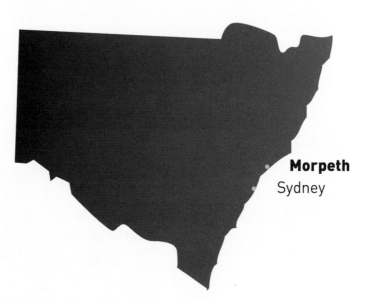

Morpeth
Sydney

Morpeth is today a small town about two hours' drive north of Sydney. The town of Morpeth grew from an original 2000 acres of land given to an English army officer, Lieutenant Edward Close (1790-1866), in 1821. During the 1830s and 1840s Morpeth became a major river port, due to its favourable location. Produce, hides and timber were brought to Morpeth from inland New South Wales and shipped down the Hunter River to the coast and then to Sydney. However, in 1870 a railway line reached the town, and the importance of river shipping began to decline. Today, Morpeth, with its beautiful old buildings, is a popular tourist destination.

QUESTIONS **1–3**

1 When was Lieutenant Close given the land on which Morpeth grew?

2 On what river is Morpeth situated?

3 When did trains first get to Morpeth?

→ **READ** these four advertisements for places to stay near Morpeth, and then answer **questions 4-7.**

WHERE TO STAY

Accommodation

A COUNTRY COMFORT INN, HUNTER VALLEY

The Country Comfort Inn, Hunter Valley, is a beautifully restored 125-year-old building just 20 minutes from the vineyards.

Formerly an orphanage, the Inn is set on 10 acres of landscaped gardens complete with pool, sauna, tennis court, spa, gym, billiard room, guest lounge, fireplace, cocktail bar, and two restaurants. Special packages available.

New England Highway, Maitland.

Call toll free 1800 065 064
or (02) 4932 5288

B SIESTA MOTEL

"Spend a night—not a fortune"

That's the Budget Motel chain motto. The Siesta Motel, rated 3-star, is conveniently placed at the gateway to the winery district and nearby to the historic towns of Morpeth and Wollombi.

The family-owned and operated Siesta offers airconditioned comfort and a friendly atmosphere. A free light breakfast is delivered to your suite and excellent meals are available at the Maitland City Bowling Club next door.

Quality of accommodation is assured and the tariff is the lowest in the district.

258 New England Highway, Maitland.

Phone (049) 32 83 22

C

ENDEAVOUR EAST MAITLAND MOTEL

28 modern, comfortable 3-star units which open onto the swimming pool and barbeque area. All units feature TV and videos, airconditioning. 2 with spas.

Fully licensed restaurant with cocktail bar and lounge is open 7 nights. Close to all amenities.

New England Highway, East Maitland.

Phone (02) 4933 5488

D ESKDALE COUNTRY COTTAGES

Rustic cottages secluded amongst gum trees provide quietness and privacy on 200 acres. The cottages are located on the historic beef cattle property, "Eskdale", nestled in the Williams Valley.

Each cottage is completely self-contained having 2 bedrooms, full kitchen facilities, and sitting rooms with TV and video, and offers comfortable rural accommodation to those who enjoy the delights of the country yet still wish to retain access to the city. Situated close to the towns of Morpeth, Maitland, Port Stephens & rainforests around Dungog.

Nelson Plains Road, Seaham NSW 2324.

Phone (02) 4988 6207
Fax   (02) 4988 6209

→

QUESTIONS **4–7**

ANSWER the questions below by writing the letters of the
appropriate advertisements in **boxes 4-7** on your answer sheet.

4 Which **two** places to stay have restaurants?

5 Which place claims to offer the cheapest rate?

6 For more information, to which place can you telephone free
of charge?

7 At which place can the guests cook their own food?

→ **READ** the description below of the town of Morpeth and answer the **questions 8-14** that follow.

The best way to see Morpeth is to take the Morpeth Heritage Walk. This covers about three kilometres, and takes visitors past many beautiful historical buildings. Starting at Fig Tree Hill, which has picnic facilities, stroll past the Surgeon's Cottage, built in 1845, formerly home of the local doctor, now shops. From there you will come to Morpeth Bridge, erected in 1870, which replaced a ferry boat. Opposite it on the right is the Courthouse, still in use today. Continue your walk past the historic Railway Station, then turn into George Street. Stroll past gracious houses until you come to the Church of the Immaculate Conception on your right, built of bricks made in Gosford. Continuing up George Street, you come to the shopping district; browse through the shops or stop for refreshment. Your tour of Morpeth will finish at magnificent Closebourne House, built in 1826 by Lieutenant Edward Close.

TOURIST ATTRACTIONS

A Fig Tree Hill
B Ferry Boat
C George Street
D Gosford
E Church of the
   Immaculate Conception
F Closebourne House
G Morpeth Bridge
H Shopping district
I Surgeon's Cottage
J Railway Station
K Courthouse

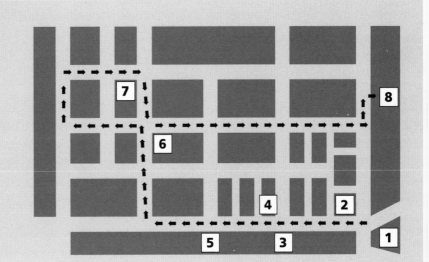

QUESTIONS 8–14

→ **USING** information from the text, fill in the names of the numbered
tourist attractions on the map. Write your answers in **boxes 8-14**
on your answer sheet. The first one has been done for you as an
example. **Note: there are more names than you will need.**

Example   **1** = _____A_____

8 **2** = _____

9 **3** = _____

10 **4** = _____

11 **5** = _____

12 **6** = _____

13 **7** = _____

14 **8** = _____

→ **READ** the information about the Numeracy Centre below, and answer **Questions 15-27**.

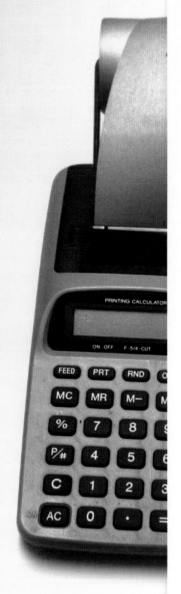

NUMERACY CENTRE

Many business and marketing courses require a knowledge of introductory statistics, computing or mathematics. If you feel inadequately prepared for your course, you can get help from the **Numeracy Centre**, which offers FREE elementary help in mathematics and statistics. Grab a timetable from the Centre and drop in when it suits you.

COURSE A

The first course available to students is a **Revision Course in Basic Maths**. This three-hour lecture will review mathematical concepts necessary for elementary statistics, such as fractions, area and percentages up to a Year 8 level of mathematics. It is not necessary to book, so feel free to drop in. This session is FREE!

COURSE B

For those students doing marketing courses, and other courses requiring statistical analysis, there is the **Bridging Course in Statistics for Marketing**. This three-day course introduces ideas in elementary statistics to provide a starting point for further developments in statistical skills later on in other courses. The course is run in sessions of three hours, in the form of a one-hour lecture followed by a two-hour tutorial. Examples will be drawn from reference books. The tutorials will be interactive where possible (e.g. drawing random samples from the population of numbered cards in class) with hands-on experience of data manipulation using MINITAB on a bank of PCs.

COURSE C

Statistics for the Practitioner is slightly different to the previous course, which must be completed before this course. This course is largely non-mathematical. It will instead concentrate on the interpretation and application of statistics rather than on computation. The statistical package MINITAB will be used as a teaching tool. This course will be conducted over two days in the form of workshops and small group discussions, with a strong emphasis on hands-on experience of data manipulation using computers.

COURSE D

A further course of interest to many students is **English for Computer Studies**. Students with English as their second language who will be needing elementary computing for their courses are encouraged to enrol in this 8-hour course. Students will learn through workshops giving hands-on experience. The cost of the course is $15 which includes notes and refreshments.

QUESTIONS **15–22**

→ **BELOW** is a chart summarising information about the Numeracy Centre courses. Complete the required details using information from the passage. Write your answers in **boxes 15-22** on your answer sheet.

COURSE	Cost	Number of hours / days	Name of previous studies required	Teaching Method
A	___15___	3 hours	none	___16___
		___17___ hours	none	lecture and ___18___
C		2 days	___19___	___20___ and small groups
D	___21___	8 hours	none	___22___

QUESTIONS **23–27**

→ **COURSES** A to D are each aimed at helping a specific group of students. Below is a list of different students. Match the students to the course that would help them most. In **boxes 23-27** on your answer sheet write the letter **A**, **B**, **C** or **D** for the number of the course, or **N** if there is no course available for the student's needs.

23 Narelle, from Taiwan, has to use a computer to do assignments in her business studies classes.

24 Joe, who left high school 10 years ago, wants to brush up on his mathematics skills before he starts his studies for the year.

25 Jenny needs an advanced course on computer graphics for her studies in Graphic Design.

26 Geoff, who has to read many articles containing statistics, needs to know how to interpret and apply the facts and figures.

27 Bob needs to know how to perform some of the basic statistic equations for the assignments in his business course.

→ **READ** the passage below and answer **Questions 28-40** that follow.

BUSINESS PLANNING

What is a Business Plan?

It is probably best described as a summary and evaluation in writing of your business idea.

Preparation of a business plan is the first and most important task for the business starter. The plan should include details concerning the industry in which you operate, your product or service, marketing, production, personnel and financial strategies.

What purpose does it serve?

A business plan allows you to think through all the factors of a business, and to solve potential problems before you come to them. It will identify strengths and weaknesses and help to assess whether the business can succeed. It is a blueprint for starting, maintaining or expanding a business. It is a working plan to use in comparing your achievements to the goals you set. It should provide information required by financial institutions when finance is sought.

How to produce a Business Plan
Step **1**: Collect Information

Gather as much relevant information as possible concerning the industry in which you intend to operate (the number of businesses already operating, the size of their operations and where they are located). Use books, industry associations, and existing business owners to help you.

Collect all possible information regarding the market/s you are aiming for (who buys, why do they buy and what are the key features the customer looks for).

Learn all you can about the product/s or services you intend to produce, distribute or offer.

Step **2**: Analysis

Read over all the material you have collected and decide what is relevant to your business idea. You may have to modify your idea depending on what your research shows. The key question to ask is:

> "Can you design a business that will earn enough to cover costs and pay a wage and reasonable profit to you as the proprietor?"

When Steps 1 and 2 are completed, you should have decided if there is a market for your product or service which is large enough and sufficiently accessible to make your new business financially worthwhile. Now you are ready to commit your plan to paper.

Step **3**: Strategy Formulation

Decide how the business will operate. You should describe how the business will be managed, and the staff and organisational structure that will be in place. Diagrams may be useful to show how these areas will work. Don't forget to include the areas of responsibility for each member of staff. This is especially important if some of your staff will be family members.

There are three further parts that go together to make a comprehensive business plan:

- A Marketing Plan, which includes location, method of selling, packaging, pricing and so on. In all these areas you must be aware of consumer trends to make sure that your business does not become outdated or irrelevant.

- An Operational Plan, which describes the day-to-day running of the business. You should include supply sources, cost and quantities of materials, processes, equipment and methods of extending the services or products offered.

- A Financial Plan, which is a master budget for the operation and includes:
  - cash flow forecast
  - balance sheet
  - profit and loss statement
  - sources of finance
  - sales forecast and target.

The financial aspects of the plan are most important and you should develop or access financial skills to make sure this part of your plan is accurate and realistic. Don't forget set-up costs and the money needed to see you through an initial period of low cash flow when calculating your first year's budget.

Update your Business Plan

Nothing remains constant in business; circumstances change, markets change, fashions change, methods change.

From time-to-time you must check your sources of information and reassess your business plan. What is relevant when you start is not necessarily so in five years' time. You may also need to revise targets and budgets if external factors (such as interest rates) vary.

Keep your information up-to-date and be prepared to change as circumstances demand. A business plan should be thought of as flexible, not fixed. If you use these steps to develop a business plan, changing it according to circumstances, you will be well on the way to a successful business.

QUESTIONS **28–34**

DO the following statements agree with the views of the writer in the passage "Business Planning?"
In **boxes 28-34** on your answer sheet write

YES	if the statement agrees with the writer
NO	if the statement does not agree with the writer
NOT GIVEN	if there is no information about this in the passage

28   A business plan must be written down.

29   Creating a business plan is only necessary for a new business.

30   A business plan should include a diagram of your proposed office or shop layout.

31   A business should generate enough money to pay salaries, and some profit to the owner.

32   The roles of family members in the business must be clearly defined in the business plan.

33   You should expect not to earn much money in the first year.

34   Once a business plan is finished, no further changes will need to be made to it.

QUESTIONS **35–40**

THE text describes how to make a business plan. Choose the correct word or phrase from the box to complete the following flow chart of how to make a business plan. Write its **letter** in **boxes 35–40** on your answer sheet.

35

Sources: books, industry associations, other people

ANALYSE INFORMATION

Ask: **36**

37

Areas to describe:

- **38**
- Marketing

- **39**
- Finance

40

A	Advertising
B	Keep your business up-to-date
C	Find information
D	Create a sample product
E	Find a good location
F	Organisational structure
G	Can I find good staff?
H	Operations
I	Create your business plan
J	Can my business make enough money?

→ **READ** the six office messages **A-F** below and then answer Questions **1-3**.

B **INTER-OFFICE MEMO**

Meeting in the boardroom on Friday, July 10 at 10 am has been changed to Monday, July 13. Same time, same place.

Please bring the notes of the previous meeting.

A

*Please call Nancy.
She will be at
818 7546 if you miss
her at home.*

C

YOU ARE INVITED

TO A DEMONSTRATION OF OUR NEW AUDIO-VISUAL
OFFICE PRODUCTS

AT

10 BARRY AVENUE

QUEENSTOWN

5 PM, JULY 28.

RSVP. REFRESHMENTS WILL BE SERVED.

E

Please note:

~~10.30~~   *12.30*

July 27

Websters Trading Company meeting,

~~30 Barrow Street~~.   *12 Jones Road*

D

MEMO TO: C. Gates

Please confirm your flights with QANTAS. We have you booked to depart August 21 at 10 am and to return a week later, arriving August 28 at 7 pm. The company will pay all expenses of this trip.

F

MEMO TO: C. Gates

Check amendments to the Ling Kee contract. Do we really want to offer 10%?

Please see me this morning at 10 in my office.

QUESTIONS **1–3**
→ **ANSWER** Questions 1-3 by writing the appropriate letter **A-F** in boxes 1-3 on your answer sheet.

1 Which message changes the time and place of a meeting?

2 Which message is probably personal?

3 Which message is from a company which is trying to sell something?

→   **READ** the Daily Work Record form below and then answer **Questions 4–13**. It records a week's work by Amanda Lee, a temporary word processor, who has been sent on a job by her employer, J & B Office Temps Pty Ltd. Some sections of the Daily Work Record form are marked with the letters **A–O**.

(A) **(B)**

J & B Office Temps Pty Ltd
Temporary Office Staff—no job too small

Level 4, 356 Elizabeth Street, Elswick
Telephone 390 5647   Facsimile 390 7733

DAILY WORK RECORD

COMPANY DETAILS	EMPLOYEE DETAILS

(C) **(D)** **(E)**

Reporting to:

Kate Shea
Office Removalists Pty Ltd
21 West Street
Box Hill

Name: (BLOCK CAPITALS PLEASE)

AMANDA LEE

Week ending:

Sunday   *14 / 1 / 2006*

(F) **(G)** **(H)** **(I)** **(J)**

DAY	DATE	START	FINISH	(LESS) BREAK	TOTAL
MONDAY	8 / 1 / 2006	9:00	5:15	:45	7:30
TUESDAY	9 / 1 / 2006	8:30	5:00	:30	8:00
WEDNESDAY	10 / 1 / 2006	8:45	5:30	:15	8:30
THURSDAY	11 / 1 / 2006	9:15	5:45	1:00	7:30
FRIDAY	12 / 1 / 2006	9:00	5:00	:30	7:30
SATURDAY	13 / 1 / 2006	:	:	:	:
SUNDAY	14 / 1 / 2006	:	:	:	:
				TOTAL	**39:00**

CLIENT SIGNATURE	ASSIGNMENT DETAILS

Please sign and also print name
(BLOCK CAPITALS PLEASE)

Kate Shea
KATE SHEA

I certify that the above hours, including any overtime, are a true and correct record of hours worked.

(K)

PLEASE TICK

Completed ☐   Continuing ☑

(M) **(N)**

J & B TEMP SIGNATURE

Amanda Lee

I certify that the above hours, including any overtime, are a true and correct record of hours worked.

(L)

INSTRUCTIONS

1. Complete this Daily Work Record using the format hh:mm (nine-fifteen in the morning = 9:15 am). If you do not use this format your hours may not be entered properly and your pay may be delayed. Work to the nearest 15 minutes.
2. Sign the completed Daily Work Record as a correct record of your hours worked.
3. When you have completed the Work Record, ask your Supervisor to check and sign. Your pay will not be processed until this is done.
4. Make a copy of the Daily Work Record for your own records.
5. Fax the Work Record back to J & B Pty Ltd., on 390 7733, by 10:00 am Monday.

(O)

TO PROCESS YOUR PAY WE REQUIRE:
Your bank details to be completed on the enclosed Banking Form.

DETAILS REQUIRED ARE:
Bank Code (BSB), Account Number, Account Name. A completed Employment Declaration Form including

your Tax Number, to ensure you are taxed correctly. Tax Certificates are sent out at the end of the financial year to your home address.

→ QUESTIONS **4–7**
USING the information in the daily work record form and the instructions, answer the questions below by writing the letter of the appropriate section **A** to **O** in **boxes 4-7** on your answer sheet.

4 Which section has the address of the company to which Amanda has been sent?

5 Which daily time record shows the longest working day?

6 Which daily time record shows the longest break?

7 In which section did Amanda indicate whether the job is still going on?

→ QUESTIONS **8–12**
USING no more than three words, answer the following questions. Write your answers in **boxes 8-12** on your answer sheet.

8 What format must be used to record the hours worked?

9 What should employees copy for their own records?

10 Who must check and sign the work record before payment will be processed?

11 What day must the work record be received?

12 What must be written on the Employment Declaration form?

→ QUESTION **13**
USING no more than three words, complete the following sentence. Write your answer in box 13 on your answer sheet.

13 Tax certificates are sent to _____

HERE and on the next page are several passages giving information for overseas students at the Language and Culture Centre in Houston in the USA. Read the passages and then answer **Questions 14-27.**

UNIVERSITY *of* HOUSTON

INFORMATION FOR STUDENTS
AT THE LANGUAGE AND CULTURE CENTRE

STUDENT INFORMATION
Campus Activities

LCC students can enjoy many sports at the university. You will find tennis and handball courts, gymnasiums, and indoor and outdoor swimming pools. At the University Centre (UC), you can play pool or table tennis. LCC student teams compete in university intramural sports. The LCC has one of the best soccer teams on campus! Please sign up and play.

You can also see films and plays, attend lectures, and go to concerts on campus. There are many international clubs where you can meet other students from your home country.

Emergencies
Weather Emergency

If the University of Houston closes because of emergency weather conditions, the LCC will also close. In the event of an emergency, all LCC students are advised to listen to major radio or television stations for announcements regarding cancellation of classes or the closing of the campus.

Teacher Emergency

Always wait in the classroom 15 minutes for your teacher. If the teacher does not come after 15 minutes, you may leave. Please go to your next scheduled class on time.

Withdrawing from the LCC

You may withdraw from the LCC if you have a medical emergency, a family emergency, or if you wish to return to your home country. If you withdraw for one of these reasons, you may receive a partial refund of your tuition. The LCC cannot refund your application fee, contract fee, insurance fee, or late registration fee. A tuition refund must be approved by the director and will be given according to the following schedule:

Time of Withdrawal	Amount of Refund
Registration week	90%
First week of classes	75%
Second week of classes	50%
Third week and after	No refund

UNIVERSITY *of* HOUSTON

Health Care

If you are ill, see a doctor at the University Health Centre first. LCC students can visit a doctor at the Health Centre. Medicines are available through the pharmacy. You should use the Health Centre as often as you need to. The Health Centre is located behind the Student Service Centre.

For some health problems, you may need to see an outside doctor. The Health Centre can help you find one. There are many clinics in Houston for minor emergencies. Some of them are open 24 hours a day. For big emergencies there are good hospitals in Houston.

All LCC students must have health insurance. You must buy health insurance through the LCC unless you have proof of another health insurance plan or financial responsibility for at least $50,000.

LCC POLICIES
Attendance and Academic Progress

The best way to learn English is to come to class regularly and to do your homework. If you miss several days of classes, for any reason, you cannot keep up with the other students. The Language and Culture Centre is a serious academic program in intensive English and wants all of its students to succeed. Therefore, students are expected to attend all classes regularly, do all classroom assignments, meet all class requirements, and make academic progress. Students who do not meet these standards may be placed on academic probation. Students placed on academic probation will meet with their teacher(s) and with either or both the Associate Director and Foreign Student Advisor. Students will be informed in writing of the terms and length of their probation.

Students who have 30 hours of absences are in danger of being placed on academic probation. Students failing to meet the terms of their probation will be terminated from the LCC for the remainder of the semester. This will also likely result in loss of student status with the US Immigration and Naturalisation Service.

Students who have 50 hours of absences will not receive a Certificate of Successful Completion and will be terminated from the program.

If a student is absent for ten consecutive days with no explanation, the student will be terminated automatically from the program.

QUESTIONS **14–20**

COMPLETE the sentences below with words taken from "Information for Students at the Language and Culture Centre" on the previous pages. Use **no more than three words** for each answer. Write your answers in **boxes 14-20** on your answer sheet.

14 In the UC students can play _____ or _____

15 You can meet students from your own country at _____

16 You should go first to the _____ if you are sick.

17 _____ must be held by every student.

18 Cancellation of classes due to _____ is announced on radio and television.

19 If your teacher is late you should wait for _____

20 If you withdraw in the second week of classes you may receive _____ of your tuition fees.

QUESTIONS **21–27**

COMPLETE the following flow charts of actions and their consequences by choosing the appropriate consequence from the list in the box, and writing its letter in **boxes 21-27** on your answer sheet. You may use any consequence more than once.

CONSEQUENCES

A   terminated from the program

B   may lose student status with US Immigration and Naturalisation Service

C   receives advice and counselling

D   may be put on academic probation

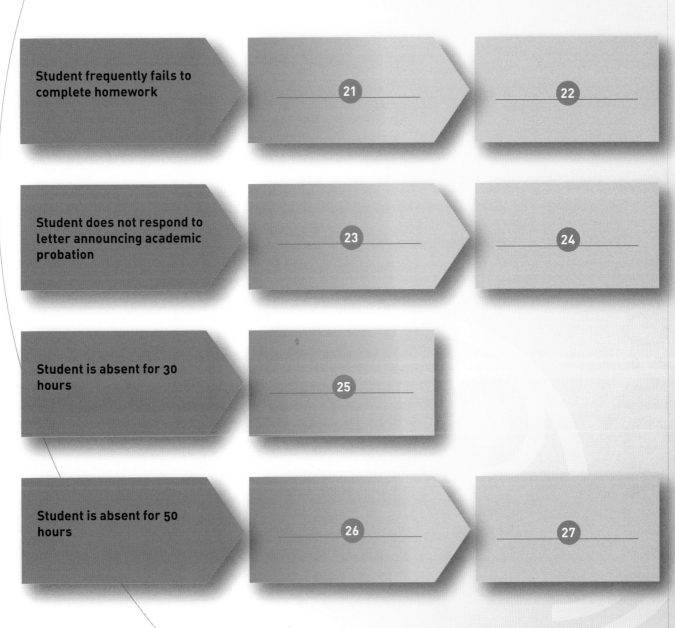

Student frequently fails to complete homework → 21 → 22

Student does not respond to letter announcing academic probation → 23 → 24

Student is absent for 30 hours → 25

Student is absent for 50 hours → 26 → 27

→ **READ** the passage below and answer **Questions 28-40** that follow.

EMPLOYMENT IN JAPAN

A Every autumn, when recruitment of new graduates and school leavers begins, major cities in Japan are flooded with students hunting for a job. Wearing suits for the first time, they run from one interview to another. The season is crucial for many students, as their whole lives may be determined during this period.

B In Japan, lifetime employment is commonly practised by large companies. While people working in small companies and those working for sub-contractors do not in general enjoy the advantages conferred by the large companies, there is a general expectation that employees will in fact remain more or less permanently in the same job.

C Unlike in many Western countries where companies employ people whose skills can be effective immediately, Japanese companies select applicants with potential who can be trained to become suitable employees. For this reason, recruiting employees is an important exercise for companies, as they invest a lot of time and money in training new staff. This is basically true both for factory workers and for professionals. Professionals who have studied subjects which are of immediate use in the workplace, such as industrial engineers, are very often placed in factories and transferred from one section to another. By gaining experience in several different areas and by working in close contact with workers, the engineers are believed, in the long run, to become more effective members of the company. Workers too feel more involved by working with professionals and by being allowed to voice their opinions. Loyalty is believed to be cultivated in this type of egalitarian working environment.

D Because of this system of training employees to be all-rounders, mobility between companies is low. Wages are set according to educational background or initial field of employment, ordinary graduates being employed in administration, engineers in engineering and design departments and so on. Both promotions and wage increases tend to be tied to seniority, though some differences may arise later on as a result of ability and business performance. Wages are paid monthly, and the net sum, after the deduction of tax, is usually paid directly into a bank account. As well as salary, a bonus is usually paid twice a year. This is a custom that dates back to the time when employers gave special allowances so that employees could properly celebrate **bon**, a Buddhist festival held in mid-July in Tokyo, but on other dates in other regions. The festival is held to appease the souls of ancestors. The second bonus is distributed at New Year. Recently, bonuses have also been offered as a way of allowing workers a share in the profits that their hard work has gained.

E   Many female graduates complain that they are not given equal training and equal opportunity in comparison to male graduates. Japanese companies generally believe that female employees will eventually leave to get married and have children. It is also true that, as well as the still-existing belief among women themselves that nothing should stand in the way of child-rearing, the extended hours of work often do not allow women to continue their careers after marriage.

F   Disappointed career-minded female graduates often opt to work for foreign firms. Since most male graduates prefer to join Japanese firms with their guaranteed security, foreign firms are often keen to employ female graduates as their potential tends to be greater than that of male applicants.

G   Some men, however, do leave their companies in spite of future prospects, one reason being to take over the family business. The eldest sons in families that own family companies or businesses such as stores are normally expected to take over the business when their parents retire. It is therefore quite common to see a businessman, on succeeding to his parents' business, completely change his professional direction by becoming, for example, a shopkeeper.

H   On the job, working relationships tend to be very close because of the long hours of work and years of service in common. Social life in fact is frequently based on the workplace. Restaurants and **nomi-ya**, "pubs", are always crowded at night with people enjoying an evening out with their colleagues. Many companies organise trips and sports days for their employees. Senior staff often play the role of mentor. This may mean becoming involved in the lives of junior staff in such things as marriage and the children's education.

I   The average age of retirement is between 55 and 60. For most Westerners, retirement may be an eagerly awaited time to undertake such things as travel and hobbies. Many Japanese, however, simply cannot get used to the freedom of retirement and they look for ways of constructively using their time. Many look for new jobs, feeling that if they do not work they will be abandoned by society. This has recently led to the development in some municipalities of municipal job centres which advertise casual work such as cleaning and lawn mowing. Given that Japan is facing the problem of an increasingly ageing society, such activities may be vital in the future.

QUESTIONS **28–35**

→ **THE reading passage** has nine paragraphs marked **A** to **I**. Match each of the topics i to ix below with one of the paragraphs **A-I** and write the appropriate letter in **boxes 28-35** on your answer sheet.

Example

Topic i: How new employees are used in a company

C

28   Topic ii: Women and Japanese companies

29   Topic iii: Why men sometimes resign from Japanese companies

30   Topic iv: Permanency in employment in Japan

31   Topic v: Recruiting season: who, when and where?

32   Topic vi: The social aspect of work

33   Topic vii: The salary structure

34   Topic viii: The recruitment strategy of foreign firms

35   Topic ix: Japanese people after retirement

QUESTIONS **36–38**

→ **COMPLETE** the sentences below with words taken from the reading passage. Use **no more than three words** for each answer. Write your answers in **boxes 36-38** on your answer sheet.

36 Japanese employers believe that moving professionals within companies and listening to workers' views leads to

_____

37 Employees receive their wages monthly and a bonus

_____

38 Japanese workers often form close personal relationships and older staff may even become a _____ to junior staff.

QUESTIONS **39–40**

→ **CHOOSE** the appropriate letter **A-D** and write it in **boxes 39-40** on your answer sheet.

39 Foreign firms are keen to employ Japanese women because

A the women are more intelligent than men
B the women who apply show more potential than the men who apply
C the women will be only short-term employees
D the women prefer guaranteed security.

40 Japanese people continue to work after retirement because

A they need the income
B they miss working
C they assist in the family business
D they have no status outside employment.

READ the following notice and answer **Questions 1-6**

ART GALLERY

The Art Gallery's mission is to bring diverse forms
of art and craft to the people of this city.

NEW YEAR FESTIVITIES

A multimedia exhibition from the four corners of the earth
On show in the Hanson Theatre, Level 2, Main Building
Free
Opens January 1, closes March 20

THE ART OF THE EARLY WEST

American art of the westward expansion
On show in the South Gallery, Level 3
$15 adults, $5.00 for members, $4.50 for students
Opens March 13, closes June 30

GREEK OLYMPIC SCULPTURE

A historical exhibit of work by ancient artists
In the North Gallery
$10 adults, $8.00 for members, $6.00 for students
Opens July 1, closes August 7

DEVELOPMENTAL ART

Work by gifted local school children
On show in the East Gallery
$2.00. Donations may be left in the box at the exit, and will be
gratefully received.
Opens July 25, closes September 30

Headsets are available for the Greek Olympic Sculpture only.
A fee of $6.00 per adult, $5.00 for members and $4.50 for students will be charged.

QUESTIONS **1–6**

→ **USING no more than three words or numbers** answer the questions below. Write your answers in **boxes 1-6** on your answer sheet.

Example

How much will it cost a student to see the Greek Olympic Sulpture?

$6.00

1 Which exhibition can you visit in late August?

_____

2 A student would like a headset for the Greek Olympic Sculpture. How much will it cost?

_____

3 Which exhibition shows the work of young people?

_____

4 How much must a member pay to see the exhibition of art from the United States?

_____

5 In which location would you find the oldest exhibits?

_____

6 Which exhibit could a large group see most cheaply?

_____

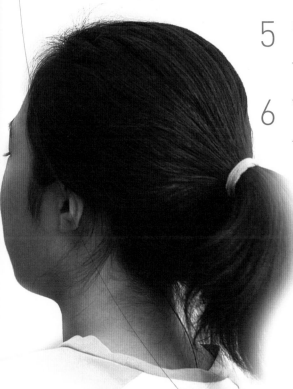

→ **READ** the extract below from the service directory of a Motorists' Association and answer **Questios 7-11**.

Call our main number **9292 9222** then call these extensions

MEMBER SERVICES, ROAD SERVICE AND INSURANCE

All insurance enquiries	**133**

Credit card payments   **344**
Visa, Mastercard for
membership and insurance policies
(open 24 hours, 7 days)

Teleclaims   **123**
For motor vehicle claims
(open 24 hours, 7 days)

HELPLINE

Road Service   **114**
(open 24 hours, 7 days)

HOME SECURITY	**553**
Alarm systems	**554**

TECHNICAL ADVICE   **443**
(8.30 am to 5 pm, Monday to Friday,
8.30 am to 11 am Saturday)
For road tests, car buying, advice and
assistance on motoring problems.
Local call charge.

Child restraint enquiries   **632**

Recorded road report   **222**
for major highways

VEHICLE INSPECTIONS
(7 am to 10 pm)   **1 300 362 802**

FINANCIAL SERVICES
(8.30 am to 5 pm, Monday to Friday,
8.30 am to 11 am Saturday)

Home Loans	**701**
Life Insurance	**976**
Personal Loans	**978**

LEGAL ADVICE
(8.30 am to 5 pm, Monday to Friday)

Sydney	**191**
Newcastle	**132**
Wollongong	**132**
Canberra	**426**

SMASH REPAIRS   **900**
Repairs guaranteed for life,
(7.30 am to 5 pm, Monday to Friday)

Batteries   **111**

DRIVE TRAVEL   **122**
Local touring information
and attraction tickets

SERVICE (HEARING IMPAIRED)

Road Service	**317**
Insurance enquiries	**728**

PREPARE FOR IELTS: General Training   UTS:INSEARCH

READING

QUESTIONS **7–11**

→ **ANSWER** the questions by writing the appropriate **extension numbers** in **boxes 7-11** on your answer sheet.

What extension should you call if:

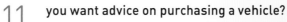

Example you want to pay your bill by Visa card?

344

7 you want to find out about a baby's car seat?

8 you feel cheated by a repair shop near your home in Newcastle?

9 you have trouble hearing and you need road service?

10 you are going on a road trip and want to find out what activities are available?

11 you want advice on purchasing a vehicle?

→ **THERE** are nine paragraphs in this advice to motorists. Answer **Questions 12-15** below by writing the letter or letters of the appropriate paragraph or paragraphs in **boxes 12-15** on your answer sheet.

ADVICE TO MOTORISTS

A Always lock your car and never leave your keys in the car. Sounds obvious, but how often have you left your car unlocked while you paid for fuel at a service station or dashed into a shop? A recently-passed law will ensure that you never forget again—heavy penalties apply.

B Always lock valuables in the boot. Most car crime is opportunistic, so don't make it easy. And if something is too valuable to lose, the golden rule is take it with you.

C Thieves need little incentive. A lot of thefts from cars are carried out by youngsters after nothing more than a few dollars, so don't leave coin-holders if they can be seen from outside. The cost of repairs often far outweighs the value of what is stolen.

D At night, always try to park in a brightly-lit area where your vehicle can be seen by passers-by. Poorly-lit streets are the thief's favourite hunting ground.

E Never park where you can see broken glass from car windows on the ground. Thieves are creatures of habit and will return to the scene of past successes.

F Install a car alarm.

G Where available, use car parks that are well lit and have boom gates. Don't leave your parking ticket in the car.

H In high-risk areas leave your glove box and ashtray open to show thieves that there is nothing in the car worth stealing.

I Don't buy goods offered for sale if the price seems suspiciously low. Chances are the goods have been stolen.

QUESTIONS **12–15**

Example Which paragraph suggests you add extra equipment to the car?

F

12 Which **two** paragraphs advise you how to show there is nothing to steal from the car?

13 Which **two** paragraphs give advice about good places to park?

14 Which paragraph warns about the effects of a new law?

15 Which paragraph tells the reader how to protect valuable items?

→ **READ** the passage below, and answer the **Questions 16-20** that follow.

HOW TO USE THE
LANGUAGE RESOURCE CENTRE (LRC)

General LRC rules

We have a number of simple rules to help you use the LRC. Please cooperate and enjoy your visit with us.

- **No eating or drinking**
- **No copying of audio cassettes**

Please work quietly. This is a library and many students are studying for exams.

Using the LRC

- You can use the LRC either on your own during self-access times or you may use it with your teacher as part of a lesson.
- If you use it as a self-access student you must scan your borrower barcode (issued by the library staff) when entering and leaving. The LRC is for use by Language Centre students only.
- All bags must be put in the bag-rack.
- Always work quietly.

Photocopying

We have a photocopier available. Please ask the library staff to help you. The cost is 20c for one A4 sheet.

Borrowing from the LRC

Language Centre students are permitted to borrow materials from the library. Other schools' students must use the facilities at their own schools.

Full-time students: Give your photo-ID card to the librarian and you will get an LRC number.

Part-time students: You will need to bring your $50.00 deposit receipt from the cashier. When your course finishes, bring your library card back and your deposit will be refunded in cash.

Loans

Language students can borrow up to four items (of which no more than two can be kits) at one time. Kits are bags containing book(s) plus cassette(s).

All teacher trainee students may borrow up to three items:

- IELTS materials   1 week
- Listening kits   1 week
- Most other books   2 weeks

Books marked REF in *red* are reference books and cannot be taken out of the library. Books marked REF in *green* may be removed by staff only.

Renewals

Most items can be renewed once. IELTS materials cannot be renewed.

QUESTIONS **16-20**

→ **USE no more than three words or numbers** from the passage to answer the questions below.

Write your answers in **boxes 16-20** on your answer sheet.

16 Which students may use the LRC?

17 What must full-time students show in order to receive an LRC number?

18 How will part-time students' deposits be refunded?

19 What mark shows a book cannot be removed from the library?

20 What materials must be returned after one borrowing period?

→ **READ** the passage below about the Buddy Peer Support Scheme, and answer **Questions 21–28** that follow.

INTERNATIONAL BUSINESS INSTITUTE
BUDDY PEER SUPPORT SCHEME

Think back to your first days and weeks in a new country. Were there times when you had questions that you wished you could ask a friend? Or when you wanted to have a chat about how you were feeling?

To help new students, the International Business Institute (IBI) plans to set up a Buddy Peer Support Scheme. The scheme will help new students meet current students at IBI who can provide them with some friendly company during their first months in Newcastle and help them with any small problems that they may have. Often, buddies may not be able to solve the problem, but they may know who can help.

What's in it for you?

We believe that being a buddy will be rewarding in several ways. As a volunteer, it will be personally satisfying to know that you are able to help new students. However, it will also help you to make contacts that may be valuable in your future academic and professional lives. If you are an overseas student, it will give you another opportunity to practise speaking English. Lastly and most importantly, we hope that it will be enjoyable for you to be a buddy!

Responsibilities of buddies

1 Telephone and arrange to make contact with the new student.

2 Meet the student and show him/her around the campus and the local area. Meet for coffee, perhaps. Answer questions about living in Newcastle and administration procedures at IBI. (We will give you a checklist of things to mention when we send you the new student's name and telephone number).

3 Arrange to meet the new student one morning or afternoon one weekend early in the semester, and take the student to places that you enjoy in Newcastle.

4 Be prepared to take phone calls from the new student to answer further questions that he/she may have from time to time. Meet to explain information to the new student in person, if required.

5 You will be matched to an individual new student. However, if you have friends who are also buddies, you might prefer to form a support group together. This would mean that you meet the new students as a group rather than one-on-one.

6   Being a buddy is voluntary. There is no "requirement" to provide assistance beyond the help outlined above. However, we hope that the buddy and new students will enjoy each other's company and continue to meet each other.

Please note that if you agree to become a peer support buddy, you will be expected to fulfil your role conscientiously and cheerfully. It will be important to be considerate and reliable so that our student can feel confident of your support.

7   When you agree to act as a buddy for a particular term, your commitment covers that term only. For example, if you act as a buddy for Term 2, and would prefer to be free in the following term, there is no obligation to continue as a buddy in Term 3. Of course, we hope that you will want to assist every term.

QUESTIONS 21–28

→ **READ** the statements below. In **boxes 21-28** on the answer sheet write

TRUE	if the statement is true
FALSE	if the statement is false
NOT GIVEN	if the information is not given in the passage

21   The main aim of the Buddy Peer Support Scheme is to help new students during exam periods.

22   Students will be put in touch with others from their own language group.

23   The principal reward for the buddy is making new friends.

24   The buddy is responsible for making the first move to meet the new student.

25   Buddies need to work one-on-one with the student in their care.

26   Buddies will be paid a small allowance.

27   The buddy's obligations finish at the end of each term.

28   Buddies are required to attend two meetings per term.

→ **READ** the passage below and write answers to **Questions 29–40** which follow in **boxes 29–40** on your answer sheet.

HOW BABIES LEARN LANGUAGE

During the first year of a child's life, parents and carers are concerned with its physical development; during the second year, they watch the baby's language development very carefully. It is interesting just how easily children learn language. Children who are just three or four years old, who cannot yet tie their shoelaces, are able to speak in full sentences without any specific language training.

The current view of child language development is that it is an instinct—something as natural as eating or sleeping. According to experts in this area, this language instinct is innate—something each of us is born with. But this prevailing view has not always enjoyed widespread acceptance.

In the middle of last century, experts of the time, including a renowned professor at Harvard University in the United States, regarded child language development as the process of learning through mere repetition. Language "habits" developed as young children were rewarded for repeating language correctly and ignored or punished when they used incorrect forms of language. Over time, a child, according to this theory, would learn language much like a dog might learn to behave properly through training.

Yet even though the modern view holds that language is instinctive, experts like Assistant Professor Lise Eliot are convinced that the interaction a child has with its parents and caregivers is crucial to its developments.The language of the parents and caregivers act as models for the developing child. In fact, a baby's day-to-day experience is so important that the child will learn to speak in a manner very similar to the model speakers it hears.

Given that the models parents provide are so important, it is interesting to consider the role of "baby talk" in the child's language development. Baby talk is the language produced by an adult speaker who is trying to exaggerate certain aspects of the language to capture the attention of a young baby .

Dr Roberta Golinkoff believes that babies benefit from baby talk. Experiments show that immediately after birth babies respond more to infant-directed talk than they do to adult-directed talk. When using baby talk, people exaggerate their facial expressions, which helps the baby to begin to understand what is being communicated. She also notes that the exaggerated nature and repetition of baby talk helps infants to learn the difference between sounds. Since babies have a great deal of information to process, baby talk helps.

Although there is concern that baby talk may persist too long, Dr Golinkoff says that it stops being used as the child gets older, that is, when the child is better able to communicate with the parents.

Professor Jusczyk has made a particular study of babies' ability to recognise sounds, and says they recognise the sound of their own names as early as four and a half months. Babies know the meaning of Mummy and Daddy by about six months, which is earlier than was previously believed. By about nine months, babies begin recognizing frequent patterns in language. A baby will listen longer to the sounds that occur frequently, so it is good to frequently call the infant by its name.

An experiment at Johns Hopkins University in USA, in which researchers went to the homes of 16 nine-month-olds, confirms this view. The researchers arranged their visits for ten days out of a two week period. During each visit the researcher played an audio tape that included the same three stories. The stories included odd words such as "python" or "hornbill", words that were unlikely to be encountered in the babies' everyday experience. After a couple of weeks during which nothing was done, the babies were brought to the research lab, where they listened to two recorded lists of words. The first list included words heard in the story. The second included similar words, but not the exact ones that were used in the stories.

Jusczyk found the babies listened longer to the words that had appeared in the stories, which indicated that the babies had extracted individual words from the story. When a control group of 16 nine-month-olds, who had not heard the stories, listened to the two groups of words, they showed no preference for either list.

This does not mean that the babies actually understand the meanings of the words, just the sound patterns. It supports the idea that people are born to speak, and have the capacity to learn language from the day they are born. This ability is enhanced if they are involved in conversation. And, significantly, Dr Eliot reminds parents that babies and toddlers need to feel they are communicating. Clearly, sitting in front of the television is not enough; the baby must be having an interaction with another speaker.

QUESTIONS **29–34**

→ **COMPLETE** the summary below. Choose no more than **three words and/or numbers** from the passage and answer **Questions 29–34** on your answer sheet.

The study of __29__ in very young children has changed considerably in the last 50 years. It has been established that children can speak independently at age __30__ , and that this ability is innate. The child will, in fact, follow the speech patterns and linguistic behaviour of its carers and parents who act as __31__ .

Babies actually benefit from "baby talk", in which adults __32__ both sounds and facial expressions. Babies' ability to __33__ sound patterns rather than words comes earlier than was previously thought. It is very important that babies are included in __34__ .

QUESTIONS 35-40

→ **DO** the following statements agree with the views of the writer in the passage "How Babies Learn Language"?
In **boxes 35-40** on your answer sheet write:

YES	if the statement agrees with the writer
NO	if the statement does not agree with the writer
NOT GIVEN	if there is no information about this in the passage

35   Children can learn their first language without being taught.

36   From the time of their birth, humans seem to have an ability to learn language.

37   According to experts in the 1950s and '60s, language learning is very similar to the training of animals.

38   Repetition in language learning is important, according to Dr Eliot.

39   Dr Golinkoff is concerned that "baby talk" is spoken too much by some parents.

40   The first word a child learns to recognise is usually "Mummy" or "Daddy".

READING

ANSWER SHEET

BONUS

You may **photocopy** this page.

READING TEXT 1

1

2

3

4

5

6

READING TEXT 2

1

2

3

4

5

6

7

8

READING TEXT 3

1

2

3

4

5

6

7

8

READING TEXT 4

1

2

3

4

5

6

7

8

9

You may **photocopy** this page.

READING TEXT **5**

1
2
3
4
5
6
7

READING TEXT **6**

1
2
3
4
5

READING TEXT **7**

1
2
3
4
5
6

READING TEXT **8**

1
2
3
4
5
6
7
8

READING TEXT **9**

1
2

READING TEXT **10**

1
2
3
4
5

TOTAL

READING TEXT 1

→ **READ** the following passage and answer **Questions 1 to 6**.

AUSTRALIA'S LINGUISTIC HISTORY

Aboriginal Australia was multilingual in the sense that more than two hundred languages were spoken in specific territorial areas which together comprised the whole country. Because mobility was restricted, one language group had knowledge of its own language together with some knowledge of the languages spoken in the territories immediately adjacent to their own. However, from the beginning of European settlement in 1788, English was given predominance by the settlers. As a result Aboriginal languages were displaced and, in some areas, eliminated. By 1983, about 83 per cent of the Australian population spoke English as a mother tongue. Less than one per cent did not use English at all. The pre-eminence of the English language reflects the fact that European settlement of this continent has been chiefly by English-speaking people, despite prior Portuguese and Dutch coastal exploration.

The first white settlers, convicts and soldiers and, later, free settlers, came almost exclusively from the British Isles. Some of these settlers spoke the then standard form of English whilst others spoke a wide variety of the non-standard forms of English that flourished in various areas of England, Scotland, Ireland and Wales. In addition, many spoke the Celtic languages including Gaelic, Irish and Welsh. However, speakers of languages other than English, did not arrive in the Australian colonies in significant numbers until the gold rushes of the 1850s, which attracted people from all over the world, including substantial numbers from China. The reaction of the Europeans to the Chinese led to restrictions on Chinese and other non-European immigration and eventually to the Federal Immigration Act of 1901. By prohibiting the entry of non-European immigration this Act hindered the spread of non-European languages in Australia. By the late nineteenth century, German appears to have been the major non-English language spoken in the Australian colonies. In 1891, about four per cent of the total population was of German origin.

Despite increased immigration from southern Europe, Germany and eastern Europe during the 1920s and 1930s, the period from 1900 to 1946 saw the consolidation of the English language in Australia. This process was accelerated by the xenophobia engendered by the two world wars which resulted in a decline in German in particular and of all non-English languages in general. As the Department of Immigration and Ethnic Affairs noted, the result was that 'at the end of World War 11, Australia was at its most monolingual ever: 90 per cent of the population tracing its ancestry to Britain'.

The post-war migration program reversed the process of increasing English monolingualism. The post-war period also witnessed a reversal of a trend of diminishing numbers of Australians of Aboriginal and Asian descent. Dr C. Price, a demographer at the Australian National University, has estimated that in 1947 only 59,000 Aborigines remained from a population of 110,000 in 1891. By 1981 their numbers had increased to 160,000.

Between 1947 and 1971, nearly three million people came to settle in Australia. About 60 per cent came from non-English-speaking countries, notably, Italy, Greece, Cyprus, Yugoslavia, Turkey, Germany and the Netherlands. Since 1973, Australian immigration policies have not discriminated against people on the grounds of race, and more Asian settlers have arrived, especially from South-East Asia generally and, more recently, from East Timor and Vietnam in particular. Between 1971 and 1981, the Asian population of Australia more than doubled to 8.5 per cent of the total overseas-born population. Traditional migration from Europe, although remaining substantial, declined in relative importance during this decade. The numbers of new settlers from Lebanon and New Zealand also more than doubled during this period and there was much greater migration from Latin America, Africa and Oceania.

QUESTIONS 1–6

→ **ANSWER** the questions below by writing the correct date in the boxes on the Answer Sheet. The first has been done as an example.

Although there had been many Aboriginal languages in Australia before white settlement, English took over as the main language from _____1788_____ .

1 The first period when speakers of languages other than English arrived in Australia in large numbers was in the _____.

2 In _____ the Australian Government enacted a law that prohibited all non-European immigration into Australia.

3 Figures from _____ show that at that time about four per cent of Australia's population was of German origin.

4 Even though there were large numbers of non-English-speaking European immigrants for part of this period, from the turn of the century up to _____ English was the unchallenged dominant language in Australia.

5 From the years after the Second World War until _____ almost 3 million people emigrated to Australia, with about 60 per cent coming from non-English-speaking countries.

6 In _____ the laws preventing non-Europeans from emigrating to Australia were removed, resulting in an increase in Asian immigration.

→ **LOOK** at the information in the map below and answer **Questions 1 to 8.**

THE COMPOSITION OF AUSTRALIA'S OVERSEAS-BORN POPULATION BY BIRTHPLACE

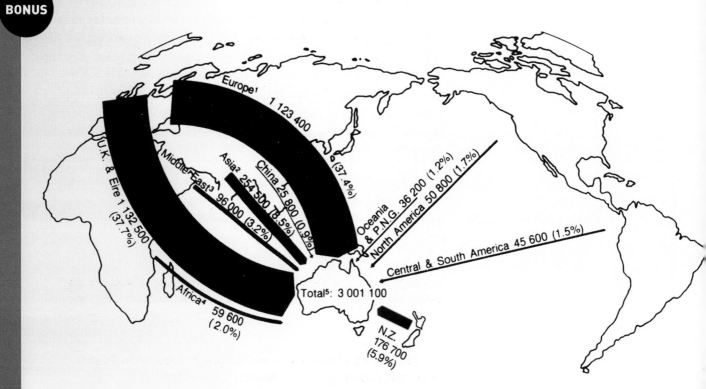

Europe[1] 1 123 400 (37.4%)

U.K. & Eire 1 132 500 (37.7%)

Middle East[3] 96 000 (3.2%)

Asia[2] 254 500 78.5% (0.9%)

China 25 800 (0.9%)

Africa[4] 59 600 (2.0%)

Total[5]: 3 001 100

Oceania & P.N.G. 36 200 (1.2%)

North America 50 800 (1.7%)

Central & South America 45 600 (1.5%)

N.Z. 176 700 (5.9%)

NOTES:

1 Principal countries: Italy, Greece, Germany, the former Yugoslavia (including—Serbia, Croatia, Macedonia). Also includes Poland, Russia, Ukraine.
2 Principal countries: Vietnam, Malaysia, Turkey.
3 Principal countries: Lebanon, Egypt.
4 The Republic of South Africa comprises 45% of the African total.
5 Non-English-speaking overseas born comprise 53.8% of the total

Source: ABS, 2004 census

PREPARE FOR IELTS: General Training UTS:INSEARCH

READING

BONUS

→ **USE** the information in the map to complete the passage below. In the boxes on the Answer Sheet, write the correct word, words or number to complete the spaces. The first one has been done as an example.

The map shows the composition of Australia's

Example   overseas-born population by 👉 *birthplace* , comprising over three million people or 21 per cent of the total Australian population in 1981.

The United Kingdom/Eire and **1**_____ were the two most important sources of migrants, with more than half of all immigrants coming from non-English-speaking countries. Thirty-seven per cent were European, principally from **2**_____, Greece, Germany and the former Yugoslavia. Non-European migration, particularly South-East Asian, has become much more significant since the 1990s.

People born in **3**_____ accounted for 8.5 per cent of the population: they came chiefly from **4**_____, Malaysia and **5**_____. Smaller numbers of people had been born in the **6**_____, (3.2 per cent), in **7**_____ (5.9 per cent) and in Africa (2.0 per cent), although of this number **8**_____ per cent were from one country. In the years 1992-93, about 26 per cent of new settlers arriving in Australia came from Asia.

BONUS

READING TEXT 3

QUESTIONS 1–8

QUESTIONS 1–8

→ **THE following passage** is a discussion on what age is the best time to learn a language. Several words have been omitted from the text. From the list in the box, select the correct words to complete the text and write them in the boxes on the Answer Sheet. Note that there are more words than there are spaces. Each word can be used once only.

debated	emotional	education
soonest	technology	examination
worst	acquire	level
only	accent	no
	controversy	question
	optimum	age

OPTIMUM AGE FOR LANGUAGE LEARNING

One aspect of the current debate on language

Example teaching in Australian schools is the ☞ *question* of when is the best time for people to learn a second language.

Language teaching within the education system in Australia has traditionally been concentrated at the secondary school **1**_____. However, many people argue that the **2**_____ age to commence language learning occurs in the early primary years or even in pre-school, when children are able to **3**_____ a language naturally with minimum interference from their mother tongue. Some suggest that early adolescence is in fact the **4** _____ time to begin to learn a language, given the psychological and **5**_____ problems many high school students face. It should be remembered, however, that many studies have shown that there is **6**_____ age at which one cannot learn a language. At 60 years, 70 years or 80 years you can still learn a language. What will cause the learner the greatest difficulty after puberty is the **7**_____. The reasons for this problem with accent have been much **8**_____.

READING TEXT 4

QUESTIONS **1–9**

→ **READ** the passage below and the table on the opposite page and answer **Questions 1–9**.

THE HEAT IS ON

Whenever the world's weather goes to extremes, scientists, farmers, fishermen and politicians wonder aloud if there is some pattern, some unifying theory, that lies behind the events. The familiar explanations are trotted out: sunspots, atomic weapons testing, too much volcanic activity, not enough volcanic activity, wayward ocean currents. All of these phenomena have been blamed in the past.

But today there is a unifying theory which many scientists believe will turn out to be the right one—the complex web of suspected causes and effects known as the 'greenhouse effect'. The greenhouse theory, now largely accepted by scientists, begins with the fact that a number of unrelated human activities—producing energy, farming, even the use of aerosol spray cans—are sending gases into the atmosphere, which may result in the globe warming. This may in turn be raising sea levels and altering the mechanics of the planet's climate in ways which will radically change its landscape. It could be happening relatively quickly, creating for our children an Earth which our parents would not recognise.

No single weather event can be linked conclusively to the greenhouse effect, but many of the recent climatic events do match the possibilities raised in computer-generated 'climate models'. The evidence of links is circumstantial but compelling.

The following are five 'greenhouse predictions':

1 The globe may be getting warmer

2 Middle latitudes may become warmer and drier

3 Dry tropical regions may become drier; wet tropical regions may become wetter

4 Fiercer, more frequent tropical cyclones may occur

5 Polar ice may begin to melt.

The Calendar of Catastrophe

INDIA
Rajasthan is ravaged by four years of drought.

1

MOZAMBIQUE
Since 1997, long-term drought.

2

AFRICA
1997–8, droughts in the Sahel region. November 1997–, drought in Central Africa and Sudan, then 28cm of rain in 10 days.

3

BRAZIL
February 1998, Rio de Janeiro, rains lead to floods and landslides, 290 deaths.

4

AUSTRALIA
March 1998, flash floods in Alice Springs after a year's rain falls in one day.

5

NEW ZEALAND
March 1998, Cyclone Bola, 2000 are evacuated, four die, 7 m waves.

6

MIDWEST, USA
April–June 1998, drought; Mississippi almost dry, 45°C recorded in Arizona.

7

RUSSIA
3 million hectares suffer drought and duststorms.

8

CHINA
May 1998, heavy rains, floods and 94 deaths.

9

TURKEY
May 1998, landslides in the Trabzon Province.

10

BRAZIL
July 1998, more floods after torrential rains.

11

CHINA
July 1998, hail and rainstorms, a forest submerged.

12

CHINA
August 1998, flash floods in the Shaanxi Province.

13

ICELAND
August 1998, heavy rains lead to seven mudslides, 280 people evacuated.

14

BANGLADESH
September 1998, floods after cyclonic storm/ tidal surge, more than 1000 reported dead.

15

INDIA
September 1998, monsoon rains lead to flooding.

16

JAMAICA
September 1998, Hurricane Gilbert, 320km/h winds, 65 killed, 160 presumed dead in Mexico, 500,000 left homeless.

17

SUDAN
September 1998, 8000 die of starvation following floods.

18

PAPUA NEW GUINEA
September 1998, a massive mudslide claims 75 lives and buries four remote villages, 600 homeless.

19

SPAIN & FRANCE
October 1998, storms and flash floods, 8 people die in Nimes where 22.8cm of rain falls in six hours.

20

NICARAGUA
October 1998, Hurricane Joan, 50 killed.

21

PHILIPPINES
October 1998, Typhoon Ruby, 500 killed.

22

JAVA
December 1998, 31 killed and 10,000 left homeless after floods and landslides.

23

THAILAND
December 1998, floods cause huge mudslides; 1000 killed, 2000 injured, 300,000 homeless. Illegal logging sanctioned by provincial officials blamed for the disaster: many people crushed by felled logs.

24

AUSTRALIA
December 1998, Cyclone Ilona strikes the Pilbara with a force almost equal to Cyclone Tracy (1974). Widespread damage but few casualties.

25

ARMENIA
December 1998, earthquake hits Yerevan, flattening cities and killing 25,000. Force equal to 10 hydrogen bombs.

26

BANGLADESH
December 1998, worst cyclone in 20 years, 1500 dead, 6000 missing, 2.5 million homeless, 200km/h winds. 4.5m waves.

27

TAJIKISTAN
January 1999, 274 killed after an earthquake triggers landslides.

28

QUESTIONS **1–4**

→ **READ** the passage headed 'The Heat Is On' and the accompanying 'Calendar of Catastrophe'. Match the examples of global climatic change below to the five 'greenhouse predictions' in the passage by writing the **number** of the prediction in the box on the Answer Sheet. The first one has been done as an example.

Example An iceberg more than twice the size of the Australian Capital Territory broke off Antarctica in 1997. It floated away, broke into three sections and is slowly melting.

Prediction Number ___5___

1 The grain belts of the US and Russia suffered some of the worst droughts ever recorded during the last northern summer.

Prediction Number _____

2 The four warmest years on record seem to have been in the 1990s (1990, 1991, 1993 and 1997). The globe appears to have warmed up an average of 0.5°C over the past century.

Prediction Number _____

3 Drought has lingered over Africa's Sahel region for most of the past twenty years, and over India's vast central plateau for most of this decade. But the models suggest that monsoons may become more intense in the wet tropics.

Prediction Number _____

4 The centre of 1998's Hurricane Gilbert, one of the most powerful storms in the Western hemisphere this century, was agreed to be of abnormally low pressure. Its most powerful gusts reached 320 km/h as it hit Jamaica, Haiti, Venezuela, the Cayman Islands and Mexico.

Prediction Number _____

QUESTIONS 5–9

FROM the information in the **'Calendar of Catastrophe'** on page 145, complete the following table of climatic disasters. Write your answers in the boxes on the Answer Sheet. The first one has been done as an example.

	Date	Event	Country
Example	*October 1998*	Hurricane Joan	Nicaragua
	September 1998	Monsoon rains	**5**
	6	Earthquake in Yerevan	Armenia
	7	Massive mudslide	Papua New Guinea
	May 1998	Landslides in Trabzon	**8**
	October 1998	Typhoon Ruby	**9**

READING TEXT 5

 READ the information below and answer **Questions 1–7**.

GENERAL INFORMATION FOR STUDENTS

 STAMPS: These are sold at the Union Newsagency at both Broadway (Level 3A) and Markets (A Block) Campuses.

 STREET DIRECTORY: A copy can be found at the Students' Association Office, Level 3A, Broadway.

 LECTURE TIMETABLES: Lecture timetables can be obtained from your Faculty Office, but if you are one of the many that suffer timetable hassles, the Faculty Clerk (at the Faculty Offices) will help you to sort out those frequent mix-ups. However, you can also see your nearest lecturer who is dubbed 'Academic Advisor' when performing this role.

 STUDENT ID CARDS: This piece of plastic allows you to borrow library books and table tennis equipment, get discounts at local stores, borrow sports equipment, and get cinema concessions at the smaller movie houses. It also acts as proof of identity where required. You will be given a card when you enrol. A lost card can be replaced by the Student Information Office, Level 4, Broadway.

 TRAVEL CONCESSION CARDS: These get you half price on public transport and they are issued upon enrolment. If you lose it or you need a replacement then contact Student Information on Level 4.

 MOVIE CONCESSION PASS: To get a discount on movie tickets at major cinemas you need a special card, available from the Union Office at Broadway.

 LIBRARY BOOK RETURN: Just in front of the Security Office at the Broadway Campus there is a library book return box which will save you a trip to the library. Overdue books cannot be left there and must be returned directly to the library.

 TRAVEL: The International Student Identity Card gets you discounts at museums, theatres, cinemas and retail outlets all over the world. It costs $8 (plus a passport-sized colour photograph of yourself) and is only available to full-time students. It is available at the Students' Association Office, Level 3A, Broadway.

QUESTIONS 1–7

FROM the information provided, answer the following questions by writing the letter corresponding to the correct answer in the boxes on the Answer Sheet. The first one has been done as an example.

Example **To replace a lost student ID card you would:**

- **A** Go to the Students' Association Office, Level 3A, Broadway
- **B** Go to the Union Office at Broadway
C **C** Go to the Student Information Office, Level 4, Broadway

1 A copy of a Sydney Street Directory can be found at:

- **A** Students' Association Office, Level 3A, Broadway
- **B** Student Information, Level 4
- **C** Union Newsagent, Level 3A

2 To purchase stamps you would go to:

- **A** The Students' Association Office, Level 3A, Broadway
- **B** The Union Newsagency

3 Overdue library books:

- **A** Can be returned in the library book return box near the Security Office at the Broadway campus
- **B** Must be returned to the library itself

4 A lost travel concession card can be replaced by contacting Student Information on:

- **A** Level 3
- **B** Level 2
- **C** Level 4

5 Do you need a special card to get a discount on movie tickets?

- **A** Yes
- **B** No
- **C** It depends on the movie house

6 Can you use your student ID card to get a half price concession on public transport?

- **A** Yes
- **B** No
- **C** It depends on the form of transport

7 If you have a problem with your timetable, you can get help from your lecturer and also from:

- **A** the Students' Association
- **B** the Student Information Office
- **C** the Faculty Clerk at the Faculty Offices

→ **READ** the following advertisements and answer **Questions 1–5**

POSITIONS VACANT

BUSY PHARMACY in Eastern Suburbs urgently needs energetic, friendly assistant. Experience required, driver's licence helpful. Ability to deal with the public essential. Great job for the right person. Apply in writing to P.O. Box 236, Elmdale South 2987.

CHILDMINDING Responsible teenager wanted to mind two school-age children Mon. to Fri. 3pm to 6pm. References necessary and experience with young children preferred. Phone 9776 5489 ah.

SALES Tired of selling all day with little to show for it? Looking to improve your sales skills? We can brush up your selling performance so that every potential customer is a sure sale. Contact Eric on 9444 3331 during business hours.

ADMINISTRATIVE ASSISTANT required for busy publishing company. Word processing skills an advantage. Must be willing to work various hours and in different sections of the company. Apply in writing, naming two referees, to Recruitment Division, Wall and Fixture Press, P.O. Box 375, Dunsmore, 2777.

EXPERIENCED WAITER required for exclusive city restaurant. Lunches and dinners. Good appearance essential, plus knowledge of Japanese an advantage. Phone 9554 9078 after 5pm for interview.

ARE YOU a bright, cheerful person? Do you enjoy creative work? Are you willing to work hard in a very pleasant environment? If so, Beecroft Hearts and Flowers, a busy florist and gift shop in a major shopping centre needs you. Experience isn't necessary but a driver's licence is. Contact Ellen, 9654 3789 after 7am.

For all your Classified Advertising phone 9797 6666
Classifieds get results!

QUESTIONS **1–5**

→ **READ** the advertisements for jobs in Part 2 of the reading passages. Answer the following questions by writing the information asked for in the boxes on the Answer Sheet. The first one has been done as an example.

Example What number should I ring to ask about a job as a waiter?

9554 9078

1 Tom is a salesman but isn't earning enough money. What number can he ring to improve his selling techniques?

2 To apply for the position in a chemist shop, should an applicant telephone or write a letter?

3 Lily is doing her BSc this year but wants to earn some money as well. What number can she ring to ask about a job in the afternoons after school?

4 What qualification is essential for the position with Beecroft Hearts and Flowers?

5 James intends to answer the advertisement for work in a publishing company. What names does he need to include with his application?

READING TEXT 7

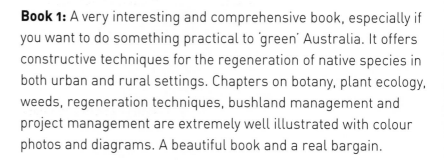

→ **READ** the information below and answer **Questions 1–6**.

CONSUMER BOOKSHELF

Book 1: A very interesting and comprehensive book, especially if you want to do something practical to 'green' Australia. It offers constructive techniques for the regeneration of native species in both urban and rural settings. Chapters on botany, plant ecology, weeds, regeneration techniques, bushland management and project management are extremely well illustrated with colour photos and diagrams. A beautiful book and a real bargain.

Book 2: Cut your energy bills and maximise the efficiency of your home with this specialised consumer guide.

Book 3: David Suzuki gives an excellent introduction to the topic of environmental science. Children aged 7 - 14 should enjoy this book with its interesting projects and activities—from testing air for pollution to making recycled paper.

Book 4: Anyone who uses pesticides in the house or garden would benefit from this book about the hazards of their use and about safer alternatives.

Book 5: If you want to avoid the plethora of specialised, packaged cleaning products (and pesticides) available and make your own from basic ingredients such as vinegar, baking soda and pure soap, this little book offers recipes trialled by the author and her friends.

Book 6: How much do you really know about the greenhouse effect? Written in a very readable style, this book fulfils the need for clear, scientifically accurate and useful information about the greenhouse effect and its impact on Australia's climate, patterns of land use and energy consumption. A sobering book, but also helpful.

Book 7: Advice on which products are the most environmentally friendly to buy, and also an interesting and comprehensive explanation of the major environmental issues affecting Australia. Find out why the critics agree this is the best book of its kind.

QUESTIONS 1–6

→ **READ** the descriptions of books in the reading passages. Answer Questions 1-6 by matching the book titles below to the descriptions. Write the number of the book in the box on the Answer Sheet. The first one has been done as an example.

Example Helen Wellings, *Home Energy Guide*

2

1 David Suzuki, *Looking at the Environment. Activities for Kids.*

2 Dr Ian Lowe, *Living in the Greenhouse. What to Expect; What to Do.*

3 Paul Rogers, *Safer Pest Control for Australian Homes and Gardens.*

4 John Elkington and Julia Hailes, *The Green Consumer Guide.*

5 Barbara Lord, *The Green Cleaner: How to Clean Nearly Everything.*

6 Robin A. Buchanan, *Bush Regeneration. Recovering Australian Landscapes.*

→ **READ** the following information and answer **Questions 1 to 8**.

TAFE COURSES

Course No: **5418**

Award: Associate Diploma

Stage I

Creative Studies I

Art theory I

Painting I *

Ceramics I *

Fibre I *

Photography I *

Printmaking I *

* The student will select two of the subjects marked with an asterisk, one will be continued as a major study for the duration of the course.

Course No: **8635**

Award: Associate Diploma

Attendance: Two years, 36 weeks, 18 hours per week (1476 hours total);
Four years, 36 weeks, nine hours per week (1260 hours total);
Available Externally

In this course, students develop the skills necessary to become professional accounting personnel. Students become proficient at understanding and processing financial data, from which they learn to produce reports, financial statements, analyses and forecasts. The accounting information, which they learn to produce, complies with institutional, legal, social and managerial standards.

Course No: **5419**

Award: Associate Diploma

Stage I

Major instrumental elective

Minor instrumental elective

Harmony & composition I

History of music I

Ensemble & conducting I

Electronic music & recording I

Concert practice I

Aural training I

Music in the community I

General education elective

Course No: 0843

Award: Certificate

Attendance: Three years, eight hours per week

This course provides the theoretical and practical training required by fashion designers in the clothing industry. On completion of the course, they should be capable of drafting, cutting and grading a basic fabric width, and understanding the processes of garment construction operations for mass production and special-measure orders in clothing manufacture.

In particular, the course provides training in metric measurements related to a variety of anatomy, body proportions and body types. Students learn to apply the concepts of design and pattern making theory to garment styling, to understand the basic colour theories, and line and shape considerations. In addition, students learn about the use and maintenance of cutting-room equipment, organisation and processes.

Course No: 3534

Award: Associate Diploma

This course is designed for persons pursuing or developing careers at management level in the sales, marketing and related administrative areas of the travel and tourism industry. It provides education and training related to those occupations in the following kinds of firms and organisations: travel agencies, tour operators, tour wholesalers, regional and national tourism organisations, and in sales-marketing facets of airlines, other carriers, hotels and other accommodation businesses.

Compulsory subjects

Geography

Economics

Tourism I

Marketing I

Business and consumer psychology

Business communication

Statistics

Tourism II

Management I

Marketing II

Financial management

Business law

Marketing III

Course No: 3519

Award: Advanced Certificate

Attendance: Three years, 36 weeks, six hours per week (648 hours total)

This course has been designed to assist the individual's advancement to the position of manager of a profit centre in a small or medium size corporation, or in the division or branch of a large-scale organisation. It aims to develop his or her ability to function effectively in one specialist area, such as sales management, understand the work performed in other functional areas, such as the finance, marketing, production and personnel departments, and direct the managerial functions of planning, organising, directing and controlling. Satisfactory completion of the course together with relevant work experience can lead to membership of the Australian Institute of Management and the Management Graduate Society.

Course No: 8510

Award: Advanced Certificate

Attendance: Three years, 36 weeks, six hours per week (648 hours total)

In this course, students become familiar with the broad fields covered by the public administration, and the relationship between the social, political, financial and managerial aspects of government. Students also develop the skills and attitudes necessary for coping with technological and organisational change. The course has been designed around five strands: Finance and Economics, Management and Organisation, Communication, Office Administration and Public Administration.

Course No: 3103

Award: Statement of Attainment

Attendance: 18 weeks, 12 hours per week, part-time, or nine weeks full-time.

This course prepares students for the appropriate examinations set by the Civil Aviation Authority. Enrolments will be accepted either for the full course or for individual subjects.

Applicants should have completed the Private Pilot Licence theory examinations.

Subjects

Aeroplane performance and operation

Engines, systems and instrumentation

Meteorology

Navigation and flight planning

Principles of flight

Flight rules and radio procedures

Course No: 0842

Award: Certificate

Attendance: Three years, eight hours per week

Trainee motor mechanics receive theoretical and practical instruction so that they may efficiently service all model engines available on the current market. An understanding is developed of the importance of maintaining the best possible quality control and engine efficiency, and a mechanic's responsibilities in relation to this concept.

Stage I

Car mechanic workshop procedures I

Engine types and fuel efficiency I

Servicing I

→ **READ** the TAFE course descriptiosn in the reading passages. Each course has a Course Number. From the descriptions given, match the Course Titles below to their description by writing the Course Number in the boxes on the Answer Sheet. The first one has been done as an example.

Example **Accounting**

8635

1 **Creative Arts—(Visual Arts)**

2 **Pilot Licence, Commercial**

3 **Management**

4 **Travel and Tourism**

5 **Public Administration**

6 **Design (Fashion)**

7 **Motor Mechanics - Trade**

8 **Creative Arts—(Music)**

READING TEXT 9

QUESTIONS 1–2

→ **READ** the following advertisement and answer **Questions 1 and 2**.

UNIVERSITY OF TECHNOLOGY SYDNEY
Kuring-gai Campus

COURSE INFORMATION EVENINGS

Bachelor of Business
Wednesday 29 August, 6.30pm

Diploma of Applied Science (Nursing)
Wednesday 15 August, 6.00pm and Monday 17 September, 6.00pm

Bachelor of Applied Science (Information)
Bachelor of Education (Teacher Librarianship)
& **Postgraduate Information Courses**
Tuesday 28 August, 6.30pm

Bachelor of Arts (Human Movement Studies)
Bachelor of Arts (Leisure Studies)
Bachelor of Arts (Tourism Management)
Contact Schools for details **9413 8497**

Bachelor of Education (Primary) Sandwich
Bachelor of Education (Teacher Librarianship)
Friday 7 September, 6.30pm

Telephone Enquiries: **9413 8200**

BONUS

→ **READ** the advertisement and answer the questions below by writing the correct letter in the box on the Answer Sheet. The first one has been done as an example.

Example **If I am interested in studying Business I should go to the university to find out about the course on:**

A   Tuesday 15 August at 6.00pm
B   Wednesday 25 September at 7.00pm
C   Wednesday 29 August at 6.30pm

C

1   **To find out about Nursing studies I can go to the information evening on:**

A   Wednesday 29 August at 6.00pm
B   Wednesday 15 August at 6.00pm
C   Monday 17 September at 6.00pm
D   Either **B** or **C** above

2   **To find out about Tourism studies I should:**

A   telephone 9413 8497
B   attend the information night on Friday 7 September at 6.30pm
C   attend the information night on Wednesday 15 August at 7.00pm

→ **READ** the following information and answer **Questions 1–5**.

Dial-It Information Services

(One local call fee is charged for each call)

Time	1194
News	1199
Sportsfone	1187
Cricket and Major Sporting Events	1188
TAB Racing Service — Day Meetings	1181
Night Meetings	1182
Weather	1196

Alpine Accommodation and Snow Report	11539	Job Line	11503
Cancer Information Service	11648	Life Be-In-It. Activities	11629
		Lottery Results	11529
Cash Management Trust Information	11625	Lotto Results / Dividends	11521
Computer line	11504	NRMA Road Report	11571
Dairy Line	1638	Ski News and Weather	11547
Defence Force Careers Line	11609	Shipping Movements (Passenger and Cargo)	11551
Dial-a-Horoscope	11635	Smoking Quit Line	11640
Dial-a-Prayer	747 1555	**Stock Exchange Reports**	
Dial-a-Record	11661	Mining	11511
Fire Restrictions Information	11540	Oil	11517
		Industrials A-H	11513
Fresh Food Line	11538	Industrials I-Z	11515
Gas Company Information	11535	**Sydney Futures Exchange Reports**	
Hints for Healthy Living	747 1133	Financials and Metals	11518
Hoyts Cinema Program and Session Information	11680	Rural	11519
		Television Programmes	11660
		Thredbo news	11544
Insurance Information Service	11570	Venereal Disease Information	11646

→ **READ** the information on the adjacent page, called 'Dial-It Information Services'. Answer the following questions by writing the correct telephone number in the box on the Answer Sheet. The first one has been done as an example.

Example

What number do I telephone to find out the time?

1194

1 What number do I call to find out the time of a movie at the Hoyts centre?

2 We want to go on a picnic today but don't know what the weather will be like. What number can we ring to find out?

3 What number will tell me if lighting a fire in the open is forbidden today?

4 I have invested money in some mining shares and would like to know what the value of my shares is today. What number can I call?

5 What number can I telephone to get help to stop smoking?

"Writing effectively in English takes lots of practice. I have a couple of pen pals in English-speaking countries and writing to them regularly, and receiving letters from them, has really helped."

UNIT THREE

WRITING

UNIT THREE
THE WRITING TEST

DURATION AND FORMAT

Writing is the third module in the IELTS test, and takes 60 minutes. There are two tasks to complete, each of which requires different text types (descriptions, general reports, discussion, argument and opinion texts) and styles of writing (from less formal to formal).

STRUCTURE OF THE TEST

The test consists of two writing tasks. There is no choice of question topics as they are both of general interest and suitable for all candidates.

Task 1 requires you to write a letter of at least 150 words in response to a particular problem or issue. This task tests your ability to engage in personal correspondence, express your opinion or needs and provide general factual information, describe, report, instruct or request. It is recommended that you spend no more than 20 minutes on this section.

Task 2 requires you to write at least 250 words. You will be presented with a topic and will be tested on your ability to respond by giving and justifying an opinion, discussing the topic, summarising details, outlining problems, identifying possible solutions and supporting what you write with reasons, arguments and relevant examples from you own knowledge or experience. It is recommended that you spend no more than 40 minutes on this section.

FACTORS IN THE ASSESSMENT

Writing scores are reported as whole bands. The performance descriptors used by IELTS examiners are confidential. Task 2 carries more weight than Task 1, so you might like to do Task 2 first. The skills on which you will be assessed include:

▷ Appropriate and accurate responses

▷ Ensuring minimum word limit

▷ Organisation and linkage of information—logical flow

▷ Range (and appropriate use) of vocabulary

▷ Correct spelling and punctuation

▷ Grammatical accuracy

▷ Sentence structures (simple, compound, complex)

▷ Examples and supporting evidence used, reasons and arguments (Task 2)

TEST TIPS

👍 Do not write a rough draft and then re-write it. You will waste valuable time. Instead, jot down a rough outline of how you wish to structure your answer and the key points you wish to make—spend no more than five minutes on this.

👍 Ensure you have some time at the end to check for small errors: verb agreements, plurals, punctuation, spelling. These things are easily corrected and affect what mark you will receive.

▷ There are **Five General Training Writing Practice Tests** in this unit. Each has two Writing Tasks similar to the kind of tasks found in the real IELTS test.

▷ Do these practice tests under exam conditions by completing each test in one hour. Keep to the suggested time of 20 minutes for **Writing Task 1** and 40 minutes for **Writing Task 2**.

🚫 **Do not** use a dictionary to help you.

🚫 **Do not** use a computer to type your work

✓ **Suggested approaches and sample answers to the tasks in the Practice Tests are provided in the Answer Key.** Please do not read these until you have attempted the tasks. Remember that these are suggestions only and that your answers may be equally valid. It is valuable to discuss your answers with other students.

→ **IDENTIFY** your Strengths and Weaknesses

Read the following statements and tick any that apply to you.

☐	I have never practised such questions before	**F**
☐	I am not sure what the question means	**T**
☐	I cannot write quickly enough	**T**
☐	I do not have enough ideas to write about	**U**
☐	I cannot say what I think in English	**U**

Using the letter next to each box you have ticked above, refer to page 13–15 for an explanation of how you can improve in these areas.

WRITING **TEST ONE**

You should spend about 20 minutes on this task.

You have a penfriend living in another country and he/she is curious to learn about the major news items in your country.

Write a letter to your penfriend. In your letter

▷ greet your friend and say why you are writing

▷ briefly describe a news story in your country

▷ explain why people are interested in it

You should write at least 150 words.

You do NOT need to write any address.

Begin your letter as follows:

Dear _____,

You should spend about 40 minutes on this task.

Write about the following topic.

 A healthy person is often described as someone who has a good diet, gets lots of exercise and avoids stress.

What should people do to stay healthy?

Give reasons for your answers and include any relevant examples from your own knowledge or experience.

 You should write at least 250 words.

WRITING TEST TWO

You should spend about 20 minutes on this task.

You are a member of an organisation which meets regularly at a particular restaurant. The most recent meal you had there was not satisfactory.

Write a letter to the manager of the restaurant. In your letter

▷ introduce yourself and explain why you are writing

▷ explain what was wrong with the food and the service

▷ suggest what he/she should do to ensure that you and your group return to the restaurant.

You should write at least 150 words.

You do NOT need to write any address.

Begin your letter as follows:

Dear Sir/Madam,

You should spend about 40 minutes on this task..

Write about the following topic.

In some countries children have very strict rules of behaviour, while in other countries they are allowed to do almost anything they want.

To what extent should children have to follow rules?

Give reasons for your answers and include any relevant examples from your own knowledge or experience.

You should write at least 250 words.

WRITING **TEST THREE**

You should spend about 20 minutes on this task.

Although you have never studied computing, you have always been interested in computers.

You have just read about a computer training course which really interests you, but it is only for people who have some knowledge of computers.

Write a letter to the college enrolment officer. In your letter

▷ introduce yourself and explain why you are writing

▷ explain your circumstances

▷ ask if a special exception can be made for you so you can enrol in this course.

You should write at least 150 words.

You do NOT need to write any address.

Begin your letter as follows:

Dear Sir/Madam,

You should spend about 40 minutes on this task.

Write about the following topic.

 What problems will your country face in the next ten years?

How can these problems be overcome?

Give reasons for your answers and include any relevant examples from your own knowledge or experience.

 You should write at least 250 words.

WRITING **TEST FOUR**

You should spend about 20 minutes on this task.

 You have lost your student identification card. You need this card to get discounts on transport and at the cinema, and to use the college library. You also need it as proof of identity to withdraw money from the bank.

Write a letter to the director of student services.
In your letter

▷ introduce yourself and explain why you are writing

▷ explain your situation and why you need a replacement ID card

▷ request a new card as soon as possible.

You should write at least 150 words.

You do NOT need to write any address.

Begin your letter as follows:

Dear Sir/Madam,

You should spend about 40 minutes on this task.

Write about the following topic.

Every country has poor people and every country has different ways of dealing with the poor.

What are some of the reasons for poverty? What can we do to help the poor?

Give reasons for your answers and include any relevant examples from your own knowledge or experience.

You should write at least 250 words.

WRITING TEST FIVE

You should spend about 20 minutes on this task.

You travel by bus every weekday, and you always use the same bus route.

Recently the bus has not been reliable. You have also noticed that the bus is dirtier than it used to be.

Write a letter to the manager of the bus company.
In your letter

▷ introduce yourself and explain why you are writing

▷ explain the situation

▷ suggest what should be done to improve the service.

You should write at least 150 words.

You do NOT need to write any address.

Begin your letter as follows:

Dear Sir/Madam,

You should spend about 40 minutes on this task.

Write about the following topic.

Every country should have a free health service, even if this means that the latest medical treatments may not be available through this service because they are too expensive.

To what extent do you agree with this statement?

Give reasons for your answers and include any relevant examples from your own knowledge or experience.

You should write at least 250 words.

"My friends and I try to speak to each other in English as much as possible. Talking on the telephone is a real challenge—you can't use body language to help get your message across!"

UNIT **FOUR**

SPEAKING

DURATION AND FORMAT

The Speaking Test is the last of the four tests in IELTS. It consists of an oral interview between the candidate and an IELTS trained examiner. The interview is scheduled either in the afternoon, after the other IELTS papers, or sometimes the following day (in large test centres).

The interview lasts for approximately **11–14 minutes**. It is recorded on an audio cassette, because in the event of a re-mark it is reviewed, and also for IELTS examiner monitoring and standardisation.

The examiner is a qualified teacher who has been trained as an IELTS examiner and approved by the British Council or IDP IELTS Australia.

STRUCTURE OF THE INTERVIEW

There are three parts to the interview. The examiner will lead the candidate through these three parts: an introduction and interview (a series of short questions and answers); an individual long turn (extended speaking) where the candidate speaks for one to two minutes on a selected topic (monologue); and a two-way discussion (dialogue) thematically linked to the topic of the long turn.

1	**Introductions** 1 min	Examiner starts the test, introduces him/herself, and confirms the identity of the candidate
	Interview 3–4 min	Examiner interviews candidate using verbal questions (Yes/No and "wh—" questions) requiring **short** answers only. Topics are familiar and concrete.
2	**Individual Long Turn Monologue** 3–5 min	Examiner asks candidate to speak for 1–2 mins on a particular topic based on written input on a task card. Candidate has one minute to prepare, and may write some notes. Topics are more detailed. The examiner might conclude by asking one or two short questions.
3	**Discussion/ Dialogue** 4–5 min	Examiner generates a discussion relating to the topic introduced in Part 2. The candidate is expected to generate **longer** responses to these questions.
	Total	11–14 min

Question Types

The examiner controls the test and leads the candidate through the three parts of the interview. There are two question types—Yes/No questions (Polar Interrogatives) and "Wh——" questions.

Yes/No questions require a **short** answer, whereas "Wh——" questions (where, when, why) require a **longer** response.

In the "Long Turn" the candidate is expected to respond to the prompts written on the Candidate Task Card.

FACTORS IN THE ASSESSMENT

The Speaking Test assesses your ability to communicate effectively in English. There are 4 Performance Descriptors to which the examiner refers to determine the candidate's IELTS Band level:

1 Fluency and Cohesion
2 Lexical Resource (range of vocabulary)
3 Grammatical Range and Accuracy
4 Pronunciation: rhythm, stress, intonation, and the sounds of English

What do these mean?

Fluency means being able to talk with normal levels of continuity, at a normal rate and easily. **Coherence** means the ability to link ideas and language together so that the speech is coherent and connected.

Do you have to stop or pause often to search for a word, to think how to express what you want to say? You do not have to speak quickly, but you need to speak smoothly and you should not have to stop to think of the correct grammar or word. Keep your language flowing smoothly and confidently.

Fluency is measured by **speech rate and speech continuity**.

Coherence is achieved by:
▷ logical sequencing of sentences – order of information
▷ clear marking of stages in a discussion, narration or argument
▷ use of cohesive devices (e.g. connectors, pronouns and conjunctions within and between sentences) to join and link information

Lexical Resource refers to the candidate's vocabulary range and the accuracy with which meanings and attitudes can be expressed.

Lexical resource is measured by:
▷ the variety of words used to discuss the range of IELTS topics
▷ the adequacy and appropriacy of the words used
▷ and the ability to manage a vocabulary gap by using other words or phrases with or without noticeable hesitation.

Grammatical Range and Accuracy refers to the candidate's grammatical range and how accurately and appropriately it is used.

Grammatical range is measured by:
▷ the length and complexity of the spoken sentences (the variety of Simple, Compound and Complex sentence structures)
▷ the appropriate use of subordinate clauses
▷ and the range of sentence structures, especially the ability to move parts of the sentence around for highlighting and information focus.

UNIT **FOUR** THE SPEAKING TEST

ABOUT **THE SPEAKING TEST**

Grammatical accuracy is measured by:
▷ the number of grammatical errors in a given amount of speech
▷ and how errors affect communication.

Pronunciation refers to the candidate's ability to produce speech which is comprehensible, and to fulfil the requirements of the speaking test.

Is your accent strong? Can you make the sounds of English clearly? Can you stress words for meaning and significance? Can you stress syllables correctly? Can you maintain a natural rhythm in your spoken language?

Pronunciation means:
▷ the sounds of English
▷ syllable stress and word stress
▷ rhythm

Pronunciation is measured by:
▷ the amount of strain caused to the listener
▷ the degree to which the speech is unintelligible
▷ and the degree of influence or interference from the candidate's first language (L1, Language One ie mother tongue)

TEST TIPS
👍 speak clearly and audibly
👍 short answers are appropriate in Part 1, but longer answers are necessary in Part 2 (the "Long Turn"), and Part 3 (discussion) where you must expand on your answers giving examples, explaining, and volunteering additional information
👍 answer the question you are asked

AFTER **THE PRACTICE SPEAKING TESTS**

→ **IDENTIFY your Strengths and Weaknesses**
Read the following statements and tick any that apply to you.

☐	I have never seen or attempted such questions before	**F**
☐	I get nervous and make mistakes	**T**
☐	The examiner asks me questions I have not thought about before	**T**
☐	I do not understand the examiner's questions	**U**

Using the letter next to each box you have ticked above, refer to pages 13–15 for an explanation of how you can improve in these areas.

→ **LISTEN** to each of the sample speaking interviews on the CD.
Using the **Speaking Skills Checklist** Worksheet, assess each of the sample speaking interviews.

You may **photocopy** this page.

1 PRODUCTION SKILLS

PRONUNCIATION	Assessment	Comments
Rhythm • Number & length of pauses	1 2 3	
Stress	1 2 3	
Intonation	1 2 3	
Sounds	1 2 3	

2 COMMUNICATION SKILLS

SPEAKING	Assessment	Comments
Fluency	1 2 3	
Clarity	1 2 3	
Coherence	1 2 3	
Confidence	1 2 3	
Cultural Appropriacy	1 2 3	

3 LANGUAGE SKILLS

LANGUAGE	Assessment	Comments
Grammatical Accuracy	1 2 3	
Grammatical Range	1 2 3	
Vocabulary Range	1 2 3	

1 = needs more attention   2 = satisfactory   3 = good

ABOUT THE SPEAKING TEST

183

PRACTICE SPEAKING **TEST ONE**

Listen to sample responses on CD3.

Refer to the IELTS Speaking Skills Checklist on page 183 to analyse the sample responses.

Good afternoon. My name is Andy. Could you tell me your name please? Thank you.

1
▷ I'd like you to tell me about your home town (or city).
▷ Can you tell me about the most interesting things in your home town?
▷ Could you describe places of special interest I could visit near where you live?
▷ What would be the best way for me to get to those places?
▷ Should I go there at any special time of the year?

I'd like to ask you a few questions about food and diet.
▷ What do you usually eat for breakfast?
▷ What is the most important meal of the day for you?
▷ What should we eat to stay healthy?
▷ Will people's diet change in the future?

2
Now I'd like to ask you to speak for 1–2 minutes on a topic.
You have one minute to plan your answer.
Here is a pencil and paper to make notes.
Here is your topic. I'd like you to describe a celebration you recently participated in.
Thank you. Can you start speaking now, please? I will stop you after two minutes.

I'd like you to describe a celebration you recently participated in.
You should say:
► where the celebration took place
► when it happened
► why it was held – what was being celebrated and explain how the celebration was conducted.

Thank you.
Are there many similar celebrations where you come from?

3
Now, let's talk more about traditions and celebrations.
▷ What role do traditional ceremonies play in the social life of people in your country?
▷ What traditions were important for your grandparents, say 50 years ago?
▷ Which traditions will continue to be celebrated in the future?

▷ How would you describe young peoples' attitudes towards tradition?
▷ Are customs and traditions changing these days?
▷ Why do you think this is happening?
▷ Do you think traditions and customs are affected by advertising?
▷ Do some countries celebrate traditions more than others?

Thank you. That is the end of the Speaking Test.

PRACTICE SPEAKING **TEST TWO**

Listen to sample responses on CD3.

Refer to the IELTS Speaking Skills Checklist on page 183 to analyse the sample responses.

Good afternoon. My name is Anna. Could you tell me your full name please? What should I call you? Thank you.

1

▷ Do you work or are you a student?
▷ Can you tell me about your studies?
▷ What is your favourite subject?
▷ What is your study plan?

▷ Do you have any hobbies or interests?
▷ What hobbies are popular with young boys and girls in your country?
▷ Do people usually continue their hobbies when they get older?

2

Now I'd like to ask you to speak for 1–2 minutes on a topic.
You have one minute to plan your answer.
Here is a pencil and paper to make notes.
Here is your topic. I'd like you to describe a movie which made a strong impression on you.
Thank you. Can you start speaking now, please. Remember you have a maximum of two minutes.

Describe a movie which made a strong impression on you.
You should say:
▶ which movie it was – the name
▶ what the movie was about
▶ who the main stars were and explain why you enjoyed the movie.

Thank you.
Do you go to the movies often?

3

Now I'd like to ask you a few more questions about films and movies.
▷ Are films popular where you come from?
▷ Are people going to the cinema more these days compared with 25 years ago?
▷ What films are popular with young people?
▷ Do people's taste in films change as they grow older?

▷ Has technology made a difference to the quality of modern films?
▷ How will technology be used to improve films in the future?
▷ Why have the forms of popular entertainment changed over the years?
▷ Will people still go to the cinema in the future?

Thank you. That is the end of the Speaking Test.

PRACTICE SPEAKING **TEST THREE**

Listen to sample responses on CD3.

Refer to the IELTS Speaking Skills Checklist on page 183 to analyse the sample responses.

Good afternoon. My name is Renée. Could you tell me your full name please? Can I check your identfication? Thank you.

1
▷ Do you work or are you a student?
▷ Could you describe what kind of work you do?
▷ What do you like about your job?
▷ What kind of job do you hope to do in 10 years' time?

▷ Do you play any sports?
▷ What are the most popular sports in your country?
▷ Is it better to play sport or watch it? Why?
▷ Can sport be dangerous?
▷ Do men and women play different sports in your country?

2
Now I am going to give you a topic and I'd like you to speak on it for 1–2 minutes.
You have one minute to prepare your answer.
Here is a pencil and paper to make notes.
Here is your topic. I'd like you to describe a vacation you have really enjoyed.
Thank you. Can you start talking now please. I will stop you at 2 minutes.

Describe a vacation you have really enjoyed.
You should say:
▶ where you went for the vacation
▶ who you travelled with
▶ what you did on this holiday and explain why you enjoyed the holiday.

Thank you. Would you go there again?

3
Now I'd like to ask you a few more questions about vacations and holidays away.
▷ Are people taking more holidays and travelling far away these days?
▷ Where did people go for holidays in your grandparents' time—say 50 years ago?
▷ Where do people usually like to go for a holiday away these days?
▷ Why do people want to travel, to go away, for a holiday?

▷ Is tourism having an effect on the environment?
▷ How important is the tourist dollar for the economy?
▷ Will the tourist industry grow in the next 10–20 years? Why?
▷ What do you think of tourism designed not to damage the environment?

Thank you. That is the end of the Speaking Test.

PRACTICE SPEAKING **TEST FOUR**

Listen to sample responses on CD3.

Refer to the IELTS Speaking Skills Checklist on page 183 to analyse the sample responses.

Good afternoon. My name is Debra. Could you tell me your full name please? May I check your identfication please? Thank you.

1
▷ Do you work or are you a student?
▷ What are you studying at the moment?
▷ Why did you choose to study these subjects (this program /this degree?)
▷ What do you hope to do when you have finished your current studies?

▷ How do you spend your spare time?
▷ When you go out do you usually go alone or with others? Why?
▷ Is there a particular time in the week when you prefer to go out?
▷ Do you think it is important to do some regular exercise? Why? /Why not?

2
Now I'd like to ask you to speak for 1–2 minutes on a topic.
You have one minute to think about what you might say.
Here is a pencil and paper to make notes.
Here is your topic. I'd like you to describe someone you admire very much.
Thank you. Can you start speaking now please? You have 1–2 minutes.

Describe someone you admire very much.
You should say:
▶ who this person is
▶ what this person does
▶ how long you have known about this person and explain why you admire this person so much.

Thank you. Is this person admired by others, do you think?

3
▷ What makes a person famous?
▷ What kinds of people were famous in your grandparents' time?
▷ In your opinion, is being well-known easy to live with?
▷ What kinds of people will be famous in the future?

▷ What responsibilities to society do famous people have?
▷ Do you think the children of famous people have an easy time?
▷ Would you like to be famous? Would being famous change you?
▷ Should the media be able to invade the privacy of famous people?

Thank you. That is the end of the Speaking Test.

PRACTICE SPEAKING **TEST FIVE**

Listen to sample responses on CD3.

Refer to the IELTS Speaking Skills Checklist on page 183 to analyse the sample responses.

Good afternoon. My name is Darryl. Could you tell me your full name please? What should I call you? Thank you.

1
▷ Do you work or are you a student?
▷ Can you tell me about your job?
▷ When is the busiest time in your job?
▷ If you could change your job, what would you prefer to do?

▷ What kind of music do you enjoy listening to?
▷ Do you play a musical instrument?
▷ What musical instruments do most people play in your home country?
▷ If you can play a musical instrument does this help you to enjoy music more?

2
Now I'd like to ask you to speak for 1–2 minutes on a topic.
You have one minute to plan your answer.
Here is a pencil and paper to make notes.
Here is your topic. I'd like you to describe your favourite teacher.
Thank you. Can you start speaking now? You have 1-2 minutes. I will tell you when the time is up.

> **Describe your favourite teacher.**
> You should say:
> ▶ who was this teacher
> ▶ what this teacher taught
> ▶ how long you had this teacher and explain why you liked this teacher so much.

Thank you.
Did other students also like this teacher?

3
We've been talking about teaching and I'd like to ask you a few questions about teaching and education.
▷ What are the qualities of a good teacher?
▷ What differences in teaching styles have you experienced with different teachers?
▷ Should teachers use discipline in the classroom?
▷ Can students learn from computers?

▷ Can you describe the education system in your country?
▷ When should children start formal schooling?
▷ Has education changed since your parents' day—in the last 25 years?
▷ Should education be free?

Thank you. That is the end of the Speaking Test.

ANSWERS & TRANSCRIPTS

ANSWERS & TRANSCRIPTS

LISTENING

SECTION ONE
1 10 Bridge Street
2 writing / writing class
3 Mrs Green
4 July 15(th) / 15(th) July / 15/7
5 1 / one
6 May 31(st) / 31(st) May / 31/5
7 June 4(th) / 4(th) June / 6/4
8 3 / three (days)
9 A
10 C
11 B
12 B

SECTION TWO
13 garbage
14 garbage
15 garbage
16 paper
17 charity
18 filters
19 A
20 B
21 D
22 B
23 D
24 C

SECTION THREE
25 Spanish
26 Building A
27 6:00 pm
28 Elementary 1 / one
29 August 10(th) / 10(th) August / 10/8
30 D
31 C
32 D
33 A
34 D
35 F
36 G

SECTION FOUR
37 ✔ lines for **London, New York, Sydney, Paris, Tokyo**
(All ticked= 1 mark,
fewer or more = 0;
some right/wrong = 0)
38 ✔ lines for **London, Hong Kong, New York, Sydney, Paris**
(All ticked= 1 mark,
fewer or more = 0;
some right/wrong = 0)
39 (very) / (extremely) **poor**
40 **special** (driving / priority) **lanes**

Narrator Here are some instructions regarding these Practice Listening Tests. In each Practice Listening Test you will hear a number of different recordings, and you will have to answer questions on what you hear. There will be time for you to read the instructions and questions, and you will have a chance to check your work. All the recordings will be played once only.

Each test is in four sections. Write all your answers on the Listening Module Answer sheet. At the end of the real test you will be given ten minutes to transfer your answers to an answer sheet.

Prepare for IELTS Practice Listening Tests. This is Practice Listening Test 1. Turn to Section 1 of Practice Listening Test 1.

Section 1. Listen to the conversation between Bob Wills, who is a foreign student adviser at a language school, and Angela Tung, who is a student, and complete the form.

First you have some time to look at Questions 1 to 8 on the form now.

You will see that there is an example which has been done for you. The conversation relating to this will be played first.

Telephone rings

Bob Hello, Foreign Student Adviser's office. This is Bob Wills speaking. Can I help you?

Angela It's Angela Tung here, Bob. I'd like to make a request for special leave. Can I do that over the phone?

Bob Hello Angela. You can make that request by phone—but I'll have to fill the form out. Let me get the special leave form. Okay. Here it is. Tell me your student number, please.

Angela It's H for Harry 5712.

Bob H5712. Okay. What's your address, Angela?

Narrator Angela's student number is H5712, so that has been written on the form. Now we shall begin. You should answer the questions as you listen because you will not hear the recording a second time. Now listen carefully and answer questions 1 to 8.

Telephone rings

Bob Hello, Foreign Student Adviser's office. This is Bob Wills speaking. Can I help you?

Angela It's Angela Tung here, Bob. I'd like to make a request for special leave. Can I do that over the phone?

Bob Hello Angela. You can make that request by phone—but I'll have to fill the form out. Let me get the special leave form. Okay. Here it is. Tell me your student number, please.

Angela It's H for Harry 5712.

Bob H5712. Okay. What's your address, Angela?

Angela I live at 10 Bridge Street, Tamworth.

Bob 10 Bridge Street, Tamworth. And your phone number?

Angela The telephone number's 810 6745.

Bob Thanks. What course are you doing?

Angela I'm in the writing class.

Bob Writing. Who's your teacher this term?

Angela Mrs Green—she spells her name like the colour.

Bob Thanks. Hmm. When does your student visa expire?

Angela Let me look. July 15.

Bob July 15. Okay. Which term do you want to take leave?

Angela Do you want dates?

Bob First, I have to write a term number. When do you want to take leave?

Angela In term one.

Bob: Okay. Term one. Now can you tell me what are the exact dates?

Angela I'd like to be away May 31 to June 4.

Bob Okay. I've got that. You'll miss four working days between May 31 and June 4. Is that right?

Angela Only three. I'll be away over a weekend. I'll be back at my classes on June 5, so that's three days away.

Narrator Look at questions 9 to 12.

Now listen to more of the conversation between Angela and Bob, and answer questions 9 to 12.

Bob Why do you want to take leave, Angela?

Angela I'm going to visit my aunt May. She's my mother's sister. She and her husband are my guardians while I'm here.

Bob Where do they live?

Angela About fifty kilometres from here, near Armidale.

Bob Do you have to take so long if they live nearby?

Angela My mother is coming with me. She's come for a holiday, so she wants to have some time with May, and I want to spend some time with my mother, too.

Bob Aren't you going home soon?

Angela I've applied to extend my time here. I expect to go home in twelve months.

Narrator That is the end of Section 1. You now have some time to check your answers.

Now turn to Section 2.

Section 2. You are going to hear a recording of instructions and advice which a woman called Martha has left for her friend John, who is coming to stay at her house and take care of it while she is away. First, look at questions 13 to 18.

As you listen to the first part of the talk, answer questions 13 to 18.

Martha Hello, John. Welcome to the house. I'm really pleased that you can be here to look after my house while I'm away.

Here are some things you need to know about the house. Important stuff like when the

garbage is collected. In fact, let's start with the garbage, which is collected on Friday. Just write "garbage" on the calendar on the days they take it away. Put it out on Friday every week, that'll be Friday 22nd, Friday 29th and Friday 5th. It's a really good service. The trucks are quiet and the service is efficient. The bin will be put back outside the house empty. It's a good idea to put it away quickly. This street can be quite windy. I once watched my next door neighbour chase her bin the whole length of the street. Every time she nearly caught up with it, it got away again.

The waste paper will be collected this Tuesday, that's Tuesday 19th. There's a plastic box full of paper in the front room: please put it out on Tuesday. The truck will come during the day. If you don't mind collecting old newspapers and other paper and putting them in the box I'll put it out when I come home—the paper people only come monthly.

I have some things to give to charity in a box in the front room. Would you put it out on Monday the 25th please? It's a box of old clothes and some bed linen which I've collected, plus a few other bits and pieces. Be careful when you pick it up, because it's heavier than you might expect. The charity truck will come by during the day on the last Monday of the month.

If you want to use the library, you'll find it on Darling Street. I've left my borrower's card near the telephone. It has a very good local reference section if you want to find out more about this city.

I'm sorry to say we don't have a cleaner. Oh, yes! Filters! Please would you change the filters on the washing machine on the last day of the month, which is Sunday the 31st. We find that the machine works much better if we change the filters regularly.

The gas company reads the meter outside the house, so don't worry about that. I think that's all the information about our calendar of events.

Narrator Now look at questions 19 to 24. Circle the correct answer.

Martha Well, John, I'm trying to think what else I should be telling you. As you know, I'm going to a conference in London. I hope to have a little time to look around. It's a great city! I do hope I manage to get to at least some of the theatres and museums.

I'm looking forward to all the things I have to do at the conference, too. I'm giving a paper on Tuesday the 26th and there are a couple of really exciting events planned later in the conference program. I hope to meet up with an old teacher of mine at the conference. She taught English Literature at my old high school and we've kept in touch through letters over the years. She teaches now at the University of Durham, and I'm really looking forward to seeing her again.

By the way, I expect you're hungry after your trip. I've left a meal in the refrigerator for you. I hope you like cheese and onion pie.

Would you do me a favour please? I haven't had time to cancel an appointment. It was made a long time ago and I forgot about it until this morning. It's with my dentist, for a check-up on Thursday the 28th. Could you please call the dentist on 816 2525 and cancel the appointment for me? Thanks a lot, John.

One last thing. When you leave the house, make sure the windows and doors are shut, and set the burglar alarm. The alarm code number is 9-1-2-0 enter.

Have fun! I'll see you when I get back. This is your friend Martha, saying goodbye.

Narrator That is the end of Section 2. You will now have some time to check your answers.

Now turn to Section 3.

Section 3. In this section you will hear a discussion between a college receptionist, Denise, and a student named Vijay about learning a language. In the first part of the discussion they are talking about the course Vijay will study. First look at questions 25 to 29. Note the examples that have been done for you.

Using no more than three words or numbers, complete the table.

Denise Hello. May I help you?

Vijay Hello. Is this the right place for me to register to study foreign languages?

Denise Yes, it is. May I have your name please?

Vijay Vijay. My family name is Paresh.

Denise Vijay Paresh. Okay. Do you have a telephone number?

Vijay Yeh. 909 2467.

Denise Thank you. Now, which language would you like to learn? We offer French, Italian, Cantonese, Mandarin, Spanish, Portugese ...

Vijay Ah. I'd like to learn Spanish, please.

Denise Okay. Our classes are conducted in lots of different places. We have classrooms in the city and here in this building ...

Vijay What's this building called?

Denise This is Building A.

Vijay I work near here, so it'd be best to study in Building A.

Denise What time do you want to to come to lessons? They go on for three hours, and they start at 10:00am, 4:00pm and 6:00pm.

Vijay I wish I could come to the daytime lessons, but I can't, so 6:00pm please.

Denise That's our most popular time, of course. Umm. Have you ever studied Spanish before?

Vijay No, I haven't.

Denise We describe our classes by level and number. Your class is called "Elementary One."

Vijay Okay. When will classes start?

Denise Elementary One begins—ah—just a minute—ah—it begins on August 10.

Vijay Great! Now what else do I have to do?

Narrator Now look at questions 30 to 32.

Choose the appropriate letters A to D and write them in boxes 30 to 32 on your answer sheet. Listen carefully to the conversation between Denise and Vijay and Anne.

Denise Well, let's see. First, you have to go to ...

Anne May I have a minute please Denise?

Denise Of course, Anne. Excuse me for a minute, please, Vijay.

Anne Did you file those forms for me last night?

Denise Ah. No. They're still on my desk.

Anne Oh, Denise, that's simply not good enough!

Denise I'm really sorry, Anne. It won't happen again.

Anne All right Denise. Go back to your customer. But please be more careful in future.

Narrator Now listen to the directions and match the places in questions 33 to 36 to the appropriate letters A to H on the plan.

Denise I'm sorry Vijay. What were you saying?

Vijay I wanted to know what else I had to do.

Denise Oh, of course. Please go to the building on the other side of Smith Street. I want you to go to the reception area first. It's just inside the door on the left as you enter from Smith Street. Give them this form.

Vijay Okay. Do I pay my fees there?

Denise No, but the fees office is in the same building. Go past the escalators and you'll see a games shop. It's in the corner. The fees office is between the games shop and the toilets.

Vijay Thanks. Er. Where can I buy books?

Denise The bookshop is opposite the lifts. It's right next to the entrance from Robert Street.

Vijay Your offices are spread out!

Denise Not as badly as they used to be. By the way, we offer very competitive overseas travel rates to our students.

Vijay Oh, I'd like to look into that.

Denise Of course. The travel agency is at the Smith Street end of the building, in the corner next to the insurance office.

Vijay Thank you very much. Bye.

Narrator This is the end of Section 3. You will now have some time to check your answers. Now turn to Section 4.

Section 4. You will hear an extract from a lecture on traffic management. Listen to what the speaker says, and answer questions 37 to 40. First you have some time to look at the questions. Now listen carefully and answer questions 37 and 38. Tick all the relevant boxes in each column.

Tom Fisher Good afternoon. I'm Tom Fisher, and I'll be lecturing you on traffic management this term. Before we go any further, I thought you should look at the sort of problems we've inherited—and "inherited", or received as a legacy from those before us, is just the word for our situation. Many of our major cities were built long before the car was thought of, and the road system evolved from the goat tracks followed by the early inhabitants. These we can refer to as old-structure problems, and you can take the expression "old-structure" to refer to problems which were in place before we saw the need to build efficient road systems.

Old-structure problems are easily demonstrated in London, New York, Sydney and Paris. Let's look at each city in turn. London has a most confusing road system, which is forgiveable because it's a very old city. I'll talk more about the ring roads later. New York is laid out on a grid which makes it easier to find your way around, but it's an enormous city and the sheer pressure of numbers strangles the roads. Sydney has narrow streets in the centre of the city, and the new road works are not keeping up. Paris has wide streets, but it's still the victim of old-structure problems, like Rome and Edinburgh. Tokyo is another city with old-structure problems compounded by a huge population, like New York. Cities which do not have these old-structure problems are Houston, Los Angeles and Dallas.

The thing which saves some of these cities is an effective public transport system, usually below ground. London has an old but effective underground train system known as the Tube, and a comprehensive bus and train system above ground. Hong Kong has cheap, swift and effective public transport in the form of Mass Transit Railway, buses and ferries. Paris has the Metro underground railway which carries tens of thousands of people daily, and a large bus system. New York has a comprehensive underground train system, but many people feel that it's dangerous to ride on it—there have been some nasty attacks. However, the trains themselves are efficient, so we have to call it a good system. Sydney has a good public transport system, but only part of it is underground.

Narrator Now answer questions 39 to 40. Write no more than three words for each answer.

Tom Notably absent from this discussion of cities with good public transport are the cities I nominated previously as not having old-structure problems: Houston, Los Angeles and Dallas. Let's start with Dallas, a very wealthy city in Texas which has grown up in an era when cars were considered to be essential to move about. It has an excellent road system, as does Houston, another new city with wise city leaders who insisted on good roads. However, the public transport system in both Houston and Dallas is extremely poor. As a result, travel in Dallas and Houston is easy except for peak hour, when a twenty minute run can expand to more than an hour in traffic jams. Los Angeles suffers from chronic highway blockages, despite efforts to encourage people to use public transport.

Cities with good road systems and no old-structure problems can use other methods to reduce the number of vehicles travelling together at peak hour. Flexi-time is one good method: offices open and close at different times so people are travelling to and from work at different times. Vehicles carrying more than one person can use special priority lanes which means they can travel more quickly. There are even systems to make peak hour car use more expensive, with electronic chips recording the presence of a vehicle in a given high traffic area at a given time.

So, what can we do? The rest of this course will be devoted to looking at the conflicting demands of road users, and relating the use of the private car to other aspects of the economy. Over the next three weeks we'll be discussing this in more detail ...

Narrator: That is the end of Section 4. You now have some time to check your answers.

That is the end of Listening Practice Test 1.

CD1

SECTION ONE

1 D
2 A
3 C
4 A
5 (to the/her) office
6 (his) brother
7 (by) 8:00 pm / 8 o'clock
8 City Square
9 People are funny
10 (the) new office) / Newtown / New Town

SECTION TWO

11 Mrs Brooks
12 Lee
13 May / Mai / Mei
14 002312
15 (Mr) Anderson / Andersen
16 Flat 5/10 or 5/10 University Avenue / Ave
17 818 6074
18 B
19 C
20 B
21 D
22 C

SECTION THREE

23 guitar, classical
24 drums, rock
25 violin, country
26 piano, opera
27 flute, jazz
28 hearts / heartbeat / blood (flow)
29 blood pressure / heart beat
30 calming / relaxing / gentle
31 cultures

SECTION FOUR

32 (the) patient / himself
33 smoking
34 young men
35 (the) sun
36 public health (standards)
37 healthy lifestyle choices
38 fun / a pleasure
39 warm-up (time) / stretching (exercises)
40 cross-training

Narrator Prepare for IELTS Practice Listening Tests.Practice Listening Test 2.

Turn to Section 1 of Practice Listening Test 2.

Section 1. This conversation is between two people, Tom and Mary, who are choosing radios, televisions and telephones in an electronics shop. Listen to the conversation and decide which of the items in the picture, A, B, C, or D they are going to buy. First you have some time to look at Questions 1 to 4 now. You will see that there is an example which has been done for you. The conversation relating to this will be played first.

Tom Well, here we are. There's certainly plenty to choose from.

Mary I'm finding it hard to know where to start. Would you like to look at the answering machines?

Tom Let's start there. I like this one.

Mary We have a lot to buy, Tom. We can't afford to pay $129 for an answering machine. And we can't afford to pay $127.50 for the dual tape answering machine, either.

Tom Alright. We'll buy a cheaper one then. There's this one for $89 or the smaller one for $59.95.

Mary I like the square shape of the smaller one. It'll fit neatly on my desk.

Tom And it's the cheapest. Okay. We'll buy that one.

Narrator: Tom and Mary choose the small, square answering machine costing $59.95, the cheapest available, so letter B has been circled. Now we shall begin. You should answer the questions as you listen because you will not hear the recording a second time.

Now listen carefully and answer questions 1 to 4.

Tom Well, here we are. There's certainly plenty to choose from.

Mary I'm finding it hard to know where to start. Would you like to look at the answering machines?

Tom Let's start there. I like this one.

Mary We have a lot to buy, Tom. We can't afford to pay $129 for an answering machine. And we can't afford to pay $127.50 for the dual tape answering machine, either.

Tom Alright. We'll buy a cheaper one then. There's this one for $89 or the smaller one for $59.95.

Mary I like the square shape of the smaller one. It'll fit neatly onto my desk.

Tom And it's the cheapest. Okay, we'll buy that one.

Mary Good. Now, we need to buy a telephone for the office.

Tom I'd like to get a portable phone. You know, one of those cordless ones.

Mary Are you sure?

Tom I think it's a good idea. We don't need another telephone answering machine, so we can look for a small one.

Mary I really like the one with the hinge in the middle.

Tom A folding telephone! Yes, that's a good idea. So we'll take that one. Are you ready to look at the other things we need?

Mary Yes. Let me look at the list. We need a couple of radios.

Tom I want one I can listen to while I'm walking.

Mary I know. They're just over here. I don't think you should buy the really cheap one.

Tom You mean this one? $17 is a very good price.

Mary Ah, that's true, but I believe they give a very bad sound quality. And what if you want to use a cassette? It doesn't have any space for a cassette.

Tom You're right. Hmm. Well, I really hate the ones where you have to put the small earphones into your ear.

Mary Here's one with big earphones you put over your ears.

Tom Ooh. It's expensive ...

Mary It's only $20 more than the one with the little earphones. Take it!

Tom Okay. What's next?

Mary We have to choose a television.

Tom We need one which is—ah—big enough to ...

Mary But not too big. I don't want anything larger than 48 cm.

Tom I really think 34 cm is too small for our room. That's only about thirteen and a half inches.

Mary Okay. Let's take the size bigger than 34 cm.

Tom What about another radio?

Mary How would you feel about a clock radio instead of just a radio?

Tom: I don't want a clock radio. I'm very fond of my alarm clock! But I like this radio with the curved carry handle.

Mary So do I. It's a good price, too. So, now we've chosen an answering machine, a cordless telephone, a radio for you to use when you go for a walk, another radio and a television.

Tom Anything else?

Mary No. Let's go and have a cup of coffee!

Narrator Tom and Mary go for their cup of coffee. Listen to their conversation, and be ready to answer questions 5 to 10.

Now listen to the conversation between Tom and Mary, and answer questions 5 to 10. Write no more than three words for each answer.

Mary Shopping's hard work!

Tom I'm glad it's over.

Mary Do you want to go home now?

Tom Yes, I think I'll take the things we bought home.

Mary Okay. I'll go to the office. I've got lots to do. I'll come back later, straight from the office.

Tom Okay. I'd better hurry. My brother's waiting at the house to help carry the television in.

Mary Good. I hope he'll still be there when I get home—I haven't seen your brother for ages. No, wait, I forgot to tell you. I'll be late home tonight. I've got a meeting at 5 o'clock.

Tom When do you think it will end?

Mary I'm not sure. Still, I should be home by eight. If I think I'll be later than 8 o'clock I'll call you.

Tom Okay. It's nice now that your office is in City Square. You don't have to travel very far at all.

Mary I certainly appreciate it! Taxi drivers always know where City Square is, too. By the way, are you going to watch **People are Funny** on TV tonight?

Tom What did you say? What TV show? Oh, **People are Funny**? Of course I am. I'll tell you what happened when you get home. I need something to laugh at—I'm going to the new office at Newtown tomorrow, and I'm not looking forward to it.

Mary I'd better go. Take care. I'll see you later. Bye bye.

Narrator That is the end of Section 1. You now have some time to check your answers.

Now turn to Section 2.

Section 2. You are going to hear a student arranging to transfer between English classes. She is leaving a message on the language department's answering machine. The student's name is May Lee. First look at questions 11 to 17.

As you listen to the first part of the talk, answer questions 11 to 17.

Mary Hello. This is May Lee speaking. This message is for Mrs Brooks, in student affairs. Mrs Brooks, I telephoned you last week and you told me to call back and put the details of my request to transfer on the answering machine. I hope you can hear me easily. I have the form here and I'll give you the information working from the top to the bottom.

As you know, my family name is Lee, spelled L-E-E, and my first name is May. My student number is 002312, that's 002312. I'm in Mr Anderson's class—you know, he's the one who helps out with the football team.

The next part of the form asks for my address. I'll give it slowly. I live at Flat 5, 10 University Avenue—you probably know the building, it's just near the engineering school.

The telephone number is 818 6074, and I share it with a lot of other people so it's often engaged. I'll give it to you again, 818 6074. I think that's all I have to put on this part of the form. I know you were curious about my reason for requesting a transfer, so I'll explain that next.

Narrator Now look at questions 18 to 22.

As May Lee continues her message, answer questions 18 to 22.

May Now I'll tell you why I want a transfer between classes. Mrs Brooks, I really like my teacher and my classmates, but I find it very hard not to speak in my own language. I just begin to think in English when the class ends, and I'm surrounded by other people from my country so it's natural that we all speak in our mother tongue. I have been looking around for a class where there are very few other people from my country so I will be forced to use English.

The best class I can find is the evening class which begins at 6pm. Most of the students in that class come from countries which speak Spanish, and I can't speak a word so I must use English. I have an Italian friend in the class, and she tells me there are two Hong Kong Chinese, six Spanish speakers and one Japanese student. She says most people speak English at the break, although sometimes the Spanish slip into their own language.

I checked the class list, and two students have dropped out of the evening class so there should be room for me. Could you please see if I can join the class? I'm not sure what the class number is, but the evening class I want is in Room 305 of the Trotter Building. The class I'm in now is next door to the Trotter building in Prince Tower, so it's very easy for me to find my way to the new class.

I'm not going home until late today, so could you please leave a message for me at my friend Margaret's house? Her number is 812 7543, and she has an answering machine.

I do hope you can transfer me, Mrs Brooks. If there is any more information you need please call me. Thank you very much.

Narrator That is the end of Section 2. You will now have some time to check your answers.

Now turn to Section 3.

Section 3. In this section you will hear a discussion between a tutor, Dr Lester, and two students, Greg and Alexandra, at the end of a talk about music. In the first part of the discussion they are talking about some of the students' favourite instruments, and favourite styles of music.

Complete the table showing the students' opinions. Choose your answers from the box. There are more words than spaces so you will not use them all. You may use any of the words more than once. First look at questions 23 to 27. Note the example that has been done for you.

Now listen to the first part and answer questions 23 to 27.

Dr Lester I think it's time we looked at the results of our survey. Ah. What did you find out, Alexandra?

Alexandra We're a group with very diverse tastes, Dr Lester.

Dr Lester Hm. I'm not surprised. What were the favourite instruments?

Alexandra Well, Greg loves drums. He told me he played drums when he was at primary school, and now he plays drums with his friends at weekends. They have a band.

Dr Lester Hm. Good. Ah. What do you like to play, Alexandra?

Alexandra My favourite is the guitar. However, I haven't played for years, so I keep hoping to start again. Will I go on with the others?

Dr Lester Hm. Yes, please.

Alexandra Katja is like Greg. She loves to listen to drums. She says she's not a player, just a listener. Rachel, as you know, is a violinist, so of course it's natural that she should favour the violin.

Dr Lester Hm. So we have two people who love the sound of the drum and two who like strings— ah, the violin for Rachel and the guitar for Alex. What does Harry like?

Alexandra Harry says the best instrument of them all is the piano. He claims it's more versatile than any other instrument. Emiko plays the piano, but her favourite instrument is the flute.

Dr Lester The flute?

Alexandra Yes. Emiko plays the flute too, of course.

Dr Lester Hm. Thank you, Alexandra. Ah, Greg, will you tell us the students' favourite style of music?

Greg We're really very conservative. My favourite is classical music, and that's Alexandra's choice too. Katja claims to like rock.

Dr Lester So that's a vote from Greg, Alexandra and Katja. Doesn't Rachel prefer classical music?

Greg Rachel made a choice which surprised me. She plays the violin, so I expected classical or opera, but Rachel says that she prefers country music.

Dr Lester Hm. How interesting! What's Harry's choice?

Greg Harry likes to listen to opera, and loves to go to see a performance. He says opera has everything, colour and spectacle and theatre and great music.

Dr Lester And Emiko?

Greg Emiko says jazz is her favourite music. She goes to listen to jazz every Friday evening. She also likes opera, heavy metal, classical ... but jazz is the best.

Dr Lester Thank you, Greg. I wanted to see what you all liked so I could understand your musical tastes more, and I want to move from this to a discussion of the physiological effects of music.

Narrator In the second part of the discussion Dr Lester will talk about the way music affects our bodies. Look at questions 28 to 31 first.

As you listen to the discussion, complete the sentences.

Dr Lester For the purposes of this discussion, I'm going to divide music roughly into two types: music which stimulates us and music which calms us.

It seems that music which stimulates us gives rise to actual changes in our bodies. We listen to exciting music and our hearts beat faster, our blood pressure rises, and our blood flows more quickly. In short, we're stimulated. Soothing music, however, has the opposite effect. We relax, and let the world go by. Our heart beats more gently, our blood pressure drops, and we feel calm. Um Alexandra, can you think of things which help us to relax?

Alexandra Um. Gentle rhythms?

Dr Lester Yes, in part. The melodies which help us to relax are smooth flowing and often have repeated rhythms. These rhythms are constant and dynamic, a little like the crash of the sea on the beach. Their very predictability is sedating, relaxing. By contrast very loud, discordant music with unpredictable rhythms and structures excites and stimulates us.

These two generalisations about the differences between music which stimulates and music which soothes are true as far as they go, but they are far from conclusive. We still have a lot of research to do to find out what, ah, for instance, people of different cultures hear and feel when they listen to music. This department is taking part in a continuing study on the influence of culture on musical perception, and we'll talk about that more next week.

Narrator That is the end of Section 3. You will now have some time to check your answers.

Now turn to Section 4.

Section 4. You will hear an extract from a talk about preventative medicine—specifically, how students can look after their own health. Listen to what the speaker says, and answer questions 32 to 40. First you have some time to look at the questions.

Now listen carefully and answer questions 32 to 36.

Parker Good morning. I'm Dr Pat Parker, and I'm here to talk to you about preventative medicine in its widest and most personal aspects. In other words, I'm here to tell you how the patient should wrest control of their health away from the practitioners of medicine and take charge of their own medical destiny. I want to talk about staying out of the hands of the doctor.

When the patient takes responsibilty for her or his own health—and let's decide the patient is male for now—men are in fact more at risk than women anyway—when the patient takes over his own health regime he must decide what he wants to do. The first thing, of course, is to give up the demon nicotine. Smoking is the worst threat to health, and it's self-inflicted damage. I have colleagues who are reluctant to treat smokers. If you want to stay well, stay off tobacco and smoking in all its manifestations.

Our department has recently completed a survey of men's health. We looked at men in different age groups and occupations, and we came up with a disturbing insight. Young men, particularly working-class men, are at considerable risk of premature death because of their life style. As a group, they have high risk factors: they drink too much alcohol, they smoke more heavily than any other group, their diet is frequently heavy in saturated fats, and they don't get enough exercise.

We then did a smaller survey in which we looked at environmental factors which affect health. I had privately expected to find air or water pollution to be the biggest hazards, and they must not be ignored. However, the effects of the sun emerged as a threat which people simply do not take sufficiently seriously. Please remember that too much sunlight can cause permanent damage.

Given this information, and the self-destructive things which people, particularly young men, are doing to themselves, one could be excused for feeling very depressed. However, I believe that a well-funded education campaign will help us improve public health standards and will be particularly valuable for young men. I'm an optimist. I see things improving, but only if we work very hard. In the second part of the talk I want to consider different things that you as students can do to improve your fitness.

Narrator Now answer questions 37 to 40.

Parker So now I'd like to issue a qualification to everything I say. People will still get sick, and they will still need doctors. This advice is just to reduce the incidence of sickness—it would be great if disease were preventable, but it's not. However, we have power. In the late 80's the Surgeon-General of the United States said that 53 percent of our illnesses could be avoided by healthy lifestyle choices. I now want to discuss these choices with you.

You should try to make keeping fit fun! It's very hard to go out and do exercises by yourself, so it's wise to find a sport that you like and play it with other people. If you swim, you can consider scuba diving or snorkelling. If you jog, try to find a friend to go with. If you walk, choose pretty places to walk or have a reason for walking. Your exercise regime should be a pleasure, not a penance.

The university is an excellent place to find other people who share sporting interests with you, and there are many sports teams you can join. This, unfortunately, raises the issue of sports injuries, and different sports have characteristic injuries. As well as accidental injuries, we find repetitive strain injuries occurring in sports where the same motion is frequently performed, like rowing and squash. The parallel in working life is repetitive strain injury which may be suffered by typists or other people who perform the same action hour after hour, day after day.

In this context, therefore, the most important thing to remember before any sport is to warm-up adequately. Do stretching exercises, and aim at all times to increase your flexibility. Be gentle with yourself, and allow time to prepare for the game you have chosen to play. Don't be fooled by the term "warm-up", by the way. It's every bit as important to do your warm-up exercises on a hot day as on a cool one.

I think one of the most sensible and exciting developments in the reduction of injury is the recognition that all sports can borrow from each other. Many sports programmes are now encouraging players to use cross-training techniques, that is, to borrow training techniques from other sports. Boxers have been using cross-training for years: building up stamina by doing road work and weight training, while honing their skills and reflexes. Other sports which require a high level of eye-hand co-ordination are following this trend, so you see table tennis players running and jogging to improve their performance, and footballers doing flexibility exercises which can help them control the ball better. All of these results are good, but the general sense of well-being is best, and is accessible to us all, from trained athletes to people who will never run a 100 metres in less than 15 seconds. Good health is not only for those who will achieve athletic greatness!

Narrator That is the end of Section 4. Now you have some time to check your answers.

That is the end of Listening Practice 2.

ANSWER KEY

SECTION ONE
1 ✔
2 ✔
3 ✔
4 7:00–9:00 am
5 6:00–8:00 pm
6 E
7 F
8 C

SECTION TWO
9 (The) Blue Mountains
10 Monday / Mon. / June 10(th) / 10/6
11 (the) front gate
12 8:00 am
13 (the) side gate
14 6:00 pm
15 (your / their) (own) lunch
16 strong shoes
17 11:00 am
18 First Aid kit
19 3B

SECTION THREE
20 8:00 am–8:00 pm / 8-8
21 9:00 am–9:00 pm / 9-9
22 24 hours
23 E (up to) 6
24 A 2
25 E 3
26 B and D
27 E and F
28 8:00 to 10:00 (am)
29 200 / two hundred
30 a nurse / nursing

SECTION FOUR
31 died (in 1900)
32 ten / 10
33 co-educational
34 teacher / university teacher
35 the Great War / 1914–1918
36 tolerance/debate/discussion
37 topics/issues
38 A
39 C
40 D

Narrator Prepare for IELTS Practice Listening Tests. Practice Listening Test 3. Turn to Section 1 of Practice Listening Test 3.

Section 1. You have just arrived at the student hostel where you will live during the term. The manager is explaining the rules, and another student is asking questions. Listen to the conversation and complete the form. First you have some time to look at Questions 1 to 5 on the Student Hostel Charges for meals form now. You will see that there is an example which has been done for you. The conversation relating to this will be played first.

Student Excuse me. I want to ask you about the charges for meals. Are they the same as they were last year?

Manager No, I'm afraid they're not. We've managed to keep most of them the same, but we've had to increase the charge for breakfast.

Student How much is it now?

Manager It's $2.50. It used to be $2.00.

Student I see. What about lunch?

Manager It's unchanged—still $3.00.

Narrator Breakfast costs $2.50, so the change has been written in. Lunch still costs $3.00, so the information has been ticked. Now we shall begin. You should answer the questions as you listen because you will not hear the recording a second time.

Now listen carefully and answer questions 1 to 5.

Student Excuse me. I want to ask you about the charges for meals. Are they the same as they were last year?

Manager No, I'm afraid they're not. We've managed to keep most of them the same, but we've had to increase the charge for breakfast.

Student How much is it now?

Manager It's $2.50. It used to be $2.00.

Student I see. What about lunch?

Manager It's unchanged—still $3.00.

Student Does dinner still cost $3.00?

Manager Yes, it does. We've managed to keep the prices down this year. But the best deal is the three-meal plan for $48.00 per week. We give you vouchers to present when you come into the cafeteria, and you get 21 meals for your $48.00. That works out to a little more than $2.00 a meal. The two-meal plan is also at last year's rates of $36.00 per week. We give you vouchers for that, too.

Student My sister was in this hostel before me. I'm sure the hours for breakfast used to be longer.

Manager Yes, they were. They used to be 7:00 to 9:30, but to keep our expenses down we made them 7:00 to 9:00.

Student Lunch is the way it was, though. Hold on! Dinner 6:00 to 7:30? Isn't that a change?

Manager Yes, it is, and in fact the form is wrong. It used to be 5:30 to 7:30, but now it's 6:00 to 8:00 pm.

Student 6:00 to 8:00 pm. That's good.

Manager So which plan would you like?

Student I'd like to think about it, please. I need to check my lecture schedule.

Narrator Now look at questions 6 to 8. Listen to the conversation between the student and the manager and match the places in questions 6 to 8 to the appropriate letters A to F on the map.

Student Can you tell me how to get to my room, please?

Manager Of course. You're in the new wing, which is very freshly painted and pleasant. But I'm afraid you're going to have to go to a couple of other offices before you can have the key. You're in the Admissions Office now. Leave this office and turn right and go to the end of the hall. The last office is the fees office, where you can pay the balance of your room deposit. They'll give you a receipt.

Student Okay.

Manager After you've been to the fees office come back past Admissions. You'll see a very large room at the north western corner of the building. You can't miss it. That's the student lounge, and if you go in there you can meet some of the other students and see who'll have a room near you.

Student That's good. Can I get a cup of coffee there?

Manager Yes, there's a vending machine in the corner. Then go to the Key Room, which is opposite the lift and next to the library, show them your receipt, and you can pick up your key there.

Student My luggage was sent on ahead. Do you know where I should collect it?

Manager The box room is next to the women's toilet. You'll have to get the key from the key room.

Student Thank you.

Narrator That is the end of Section 1. You will now have some time to check your answers.

Now turn to Section 2.

Section 2. You are going to hear a teacher helping high school students visiting from an overseas school to fill in a school excursion permission note. First look at questions 9 to 16.

Listen while a teacher tells you how to complete the school excursion permission note. Write no more than three words or numbers for each answer.

Mrs Brown Good morning students. My name is Mrs Brown, and I'm in charge of the school excursion next week. Please take out your

School Excursion Permission Note so you can fill it in. For insurance purposes, this note must be signed by your guardian or the group leader. First of all, fill in the name of your class. Everyone here is in 3A, aren't they? So write 3A where it says "class". We're going to the Blue Mountains, which is great, so this is the school excursion to the Blue Mountains. The day we leave is Monday that's Monday June 10.

We are travelling by bus all the way, so we don't have to worry about changing trains or anything like that. The bus will leave from the front gate at 8:00 am. I know we usually use the side gate, but because of the roadworks we will be using the front gate when we leave. However, when we return the roadwork will be complete so we'll use the side gate. We expect to be back at 6:00 pm.

It's going to be a lovely day. Your teachers will give you tasks to do when we arrive. We'll provide fruit and fruit juice on the bus, but you must bring your own lunch.

While we're on the excursion we'll be moving around a lot in some fairly rough country. Be very careful to wear strong shoes. It's very important that you look after your feet very well. Now does anyone have any questions they want to ask?

Narrator Now look at questions 17 to 19.

As the talk continues, answer questions 17 to 19. Write no more than three words or numbers for each answer.

Mrs Brown No questions? Okay. I'd just like to fill in a few more details. The bus should arrive in the Blue Mountains at 11 am. We'll have time to do the first of our tasks before lunch. The bus is not a new one, but it does carry one piece of special equipment—a first aid kit. I certainly hope we won't have to use it, but it's nice to know it's there in case we have a medical emergency.

The other class on this excursion is 3B, so I know it'll be a good day. The last time 3A and 3B went out together was a thoroughly successful excursion.

Narrator That is the end of Section 2. You will now have some time to check your answers.

Now turn to Section 3.

Section 3. In this section you will hear a conversation between Mrs Lam, a member of the staff in a large hospital, and Andrew, who is a student in the nursing school. Mrs Lam is explaining the rules about visiting hours in the hospital. Look at questions 20 to 25.

Listen to the first part of the conversation and answer questions 20 to 22. Complete the table showing when visitors may go to the different parts of the hospital.

Mrs Lam Hello, Andrew. I believe you want to know about visiting hours?

Andrew Yes, I do Mrs Lam. I have to fill this form out, and I'd like to have some idea why the different parts of the hospital have different times for visiting.

Mrs Lam I see. Well, let's start with an obvious one. Intensive care. People in intensive care are very sick indeed, and for that reason we say that visitors can come between 6:00am and midnight.

Andrew I can understand that.

Mrs Lam At the other end of the scale, our maternity patients are usually quite well, but we restrict their visiting hours from 8:00 am to 8:00 pm. We find they get very tired if we permit visitors all the time.

Andrew I see. What about the surgical wards?

Mrs Lam The doctors prefer to do their rounds early in surgical, so visiting hours are 9:00am to 9:00pm. Surgical patients are often on very heavy painkillers, and they aren't really very good company for their visitors!

Andrew But surely the visitors come to cheer up the patient, not the other way round?

Mrs Lam Of course. And often the visitors are able to help the patient a lot. That's why we allow visitors all day, the full 24 hours, in the emergency ward. They help comfort the patient while they're waiting to be diagnosed.

Narrator In the second part of the discussion Andrew will ask Mrs Lam about the people who are allowed to visit patients. Look at questions 23 to 25 first.

Complete the table showing who is allowed to visit, and the number of visitors permitted. Use the letter A to show that Adults may visit, E to show that Everyone may visit and I to show that only Immediate family may visit.

Mrs Lam Of course, it's not just everyone who can visit a sick patient. People in intensive care can only be visited by their immediate family. What's more, we only allow two people in at any time. We let children of the immediate family in to visit people in intensive care, but we don't like to do it. It's very hard on the children, and it may distress the patient. However, if the patient asks for the child, and the family agrees, that's okay.

Andrew What about children in maternity?

Mrs Lam Of course we let them in! They're very pleased to see their mothers. The rule in maternity is everyone may visit, up to six people at a time. The maternity ward is quite sociable, after all.

Andrew The surgical ward must be different.

Mrs Lam It is indeed. We don't allow children in the surgical ward because of the danger of infection, and as you know we restrict the hours. There are a lot of procedures which must be carried out on surgical patients, and we only let two visitors come in at a time.

Andrew And in Emergency, people are allowed to visit all the time?

Mrs Lam Oh yes. We rely on patients' relatives to be there for them, and we permit everyone to visit the emergency department at all hours.

However, we restrict it to three visitors for each patient. Otherwise the room just gets totally crowded.

Narrator Now listen to Mrs Lam explaining where Andrew will spend the first week of his training. Circle two letters. An example has been done for you. Look at questions 26 and 27.

Circle two letters in each answer.

Mrs Lam Now I have your schedule for the next week's observation sessions. Are you ready?

Andrew Yes. Where do I start?

Mrs Lam On Monday you'll be in male surgical in the morning, and in female surgical in the afternoon. You'll be following Dr Shay on her rounds.

Andrew Thank you. And on Tuesday?

Mrs Lam On Tuesday you will be with Dr Thomas in the morning and Dr Robertson in the afternoon. No, that can't be right ... you're with Dr Thomas in the afternoon and Dr Robertson in the morning.

Andrew Do I ever get to see Dr Kim?

Mrs Lam Yes, you'll be with Dr Kim on Thursday and Friday. She'll take you through the children's ward and through our new teenage ward for 12 to 15 year olds.

Andrew Great! I've read a lot about that new ward. Will I see the school room?

Mrs Lam Maybe another time.

Narrator Now look at questions 28 to 30.

Now answer questions 28 to 30. Write no more than three words or numbers for each answer.

Andrew And what will I do on Wednesday?

Mrs Lam On Wednesday you'll join the other students for lectures. You'll be in the Redmore Lecture Room between 8 and 10 am and later between 2:00 and 3:00 pm.

Andrew Thank you. Do you know how big my class is?

Mrs Lam The intake this term is two hundred first year students. I'm pleased to say about one third are men, which is good. Nursing used to be an almost entirely female occupation.

Andrew I know. My father trained as a nurse, and he was considered very unusual.

Mrs Lam Is he still working as a nurse?

Andrew Yes. He's working in a hospital in the country. I guess I just wanted to follow his example.

Narrator That is the end of Section 3. You will now have some time to check your answers.

Now turn to Section 4.

Section 4. You will hear an extract from an introductory talk given to a group of students who have just entered a university residential college.
The speaker is the principal of the college.

Listen to what the speaker says, and answer questions 31 to 40. First you have some time to look at questions 31 to 37.

Now listen carefully and answer questions 31 to 37.

Principal Good morning, and welcome to Scholastic House. I am delighted to see you here. It is my duty to explain to you some of the history of our college and some of the traditions which I hope you will uphold.

The idea for Scholastic House was expounded by Samuel Wells in 1898. Wells was a visionary, whose ideas were well ahead of his time. He wanted a college which would encourage friendship between people of different races and nationalities. Wells died in 1900 before he could see the college in action.

Scholastic House finally began operating in 1903 with ten students. Those students came from Asia, Europe, and the Americas. At that time Scholastic House accepted only male students, although it has been co-educational since 1963. Nine of these foundation students went on to lead illustrious lives; the only exception died tragically on his way home from Scholastic House to Sarawak. He had only recently graduated with an honours degree in Law, and he was robbed of a brilliant future.

The other nine students, as I said, led very fulfilling lives. Three became political leaders, three became doctors. Perhaps the most famous graduate became a university teacher and was responsible for the introduction of modern teaching training methods in his country. Two of the original group became senior engineers and went on to deeply influence the way the water systems of their country were exploited.

The college ran into hard times during the period of the Great War, 1914 to 1918, when the charter of the college was interpreted to mean that neither students nor staff could take part in the war effort. Many people felt that this indicated a lack of national spirit, and the walls of the college were frequently marked with graffiti. Meantime, outside the college, tens of thousands of young men went away to fight in Europe, never to return.

The college was building a reputation for learning and for tolerance of opposing views. Scholastic House debate and discussion nights were opened to the public in 1927, and have been available to anyone who wishes to attend ever since. It is a

TRANSCRIPT
Practice Listening Test 3 continued

proud tradition of the college that any view may be expressed provided that it can be defended intellectually. Over the years topics which were controversial at the time have been discussed and debated.

Narrator Now look at questions 38 to 40.

Principal As I said, the college has a proud history of publicly examining controversial issues. Why should we do this? The publicity we receive is often sensational, and there is no joy in encouraging argument for its own sake; in fact that sort of discussion just increases tension. The only legitimate reason for our behaviour is that it casts light upon the topic in question and informs the debate.

And controversial topics are the ones which most need informed attention. As the world forges ahead we often find our scientists have outstripped our philosophers. We frequently develop scientific marvels without realising their full implications. Nowhere is this more obvious than in medicine. We are now able to keep people alive far longer than before, but this medical ability must be measured in relation to the quality of those lives.

I urge you to spend your time at Scholastic House wisely. You are the heirs of an excellent academic tradition of which we can all be justly proud. It is your responsibility to continue this tradition of querying where our world is going. Progress is not always upwards.

I wish you every joy in your time here, and I hope that I will hear much well informed debate from you.

Narrator That is the end of Section 4. Now you have some time to check your answers.

That is the end of Listening Practice Test 3.

ANSWER KEY
Practice Listening Test 4

SECTION ONE
1 C
2 T
3 CT
4 CST
5 T
6 T
7 S
8 C

SECTION TWO
9 ✓
10 11:00 (pm)
11 11:30 (pm)
12 ✓
13 ✓
14 Thurs / Thursday
15 Smith Street
16 laying (telephone) cable(s)
17 (the) college grounds
18 side door

SECTION THREE
19 water wheel
20 gears
21 spray tube
22 holes
23 base
24 C
25 A
26 A
27 A
28 B
29 D

SECTION FOUR
30 hunger
31 noise
32 study
33 tense
34 tired
35 45 degrees
36 relaxed
37 chew
38 exercise
39 smoky
40 long-term

Narrator Prepare for IELTS Practice Listening Tests. Practice Listening Test 4.

Turn to Section 1 of Practice Listening Test 4.

Section 1. Listen to the conversation between two students, John and Carol. They have a list of the names of authors whose books have been given to the library. They have to classify the authors as writers of cookery, sports or travel. First you have some time to look at Questions 1 to 8 on the table now.

You will see that there is an example which has been done for you. The conversation relating to this will be played first.

John This is a great collection of books, isn't it?

Carol Very impressive. Who gave them to us?

John Apparently the donor was a book reviewer. There are a lot of books about sport. Here's one. My Life in Cricket.

Carol That's certainly sports. Who's the author?

John Peter Adams.

Carol He also wrote Journeys through Spain.

John Did he?

Narrator Peter Adams writes on both sports and travel, so S T is written against his name.

Now we shall begin. You should answer the questions as you listen because you will not hear the recording a second time. Now listen carefully and answer questions 1 to 8.

John This is a great collection of books, isn't it?

Carol Very impressive. Who gave them to us?

John Apparently the donor was a book reviewer. There are a lot of books about sport. Here's one. My life in cricket.

Carol That's certainly sports. Who's the author?

John Peter Adams.

Carol He also wrote Journeys through Spain.

John Did he?

Carol Next one is Stephen Bau.

John He wrote Summer Barbecues, Cooking for Singles, Dinners by Candlelight ...

Carol Anything else?

John No. Do you have anything by Pam Campbell?

Carol Wanderings in Greece, My Life in Russia, Travels in the Amazon, and Pam Campbell's Guide to a Successful Trip.

John Sounds like she got around! My next one is C. Kezik.

Carol He has a list of books about football. The World Cup, Heroes of the World Cup, Playing with the Round Ball, Soccer for Everyone ...

John That's enough! He was a one-topic writer. Ari Hussein, however, wrote about cooking and travel! His series of cook books is called Living and Cooking in Spain, Living and Cooking in China, Living and Cooking in Brazil. He's been everywhere.

Carol I've got a specialist here. Sally Innes on tennis. Here are some of her titles: Improve Your Serve, Tennis for Everyone, Tennis Forever!

John Meg Jorgensen has three books, one in each category: Cooking for Health, Sport is Good for You! and Travelling in Australia.

Carol A varied talent. Who's next?

John Bruno Murray. He wrote children's books—a whole series called A Child's Guide to ... and then the name of the city.

Carol Oh. You mean like A Child's Guide to London?

John Yes, that's right. He seems to have stayed in Europe. Ruby Lee, however, has just one book. It's called The Emerald Isle and it's all about Ireland. Apparently she went around Ireland on foot.

Carol Jim Wells wouldn't like that! His books are all about motor racing. Hmm. Nice photos of old racing cars. Don't you love the goggles on the driver?

John They do look strange, don't they? I think we're nearly finished. What did Helen Yeung write?

Carol Summer Menus: Food for Thought. She also did a book of Chinese recipes—Cantonese, I think.

John Okay. That's dealt with the first box. Let's stop for a minute.

Narrator That is the end of Section 1. You now have some time to check your answers

Now turn to Section 2.

Section 2. You are going to hear a talk by a student adviser who is inviting new students to a welcoming party: Look at the invitation. Tick if the information is correct or write in the changes. First look at questions 9 to 14.

As you listen to the first part of the talk, answer questions 9 to 14.

Student Adviser Hello. My name is Dave Burns, and I'm here to tell you about the welcoming party we are having for new students. Unfortunately the information on your invitation is inaccurate. We didn't have enough time to print new invitations, so I'll have to ask you to make changes.

To start with, this isn't a welcoming lunch: it's a dance party. However, the next line is true. The party will be held at Blackwell House. Is everybody comfortable with that? The next line tells you when the party will be: Friday June 15th at 8:00 pm, but I have good news: the party will end at 11:00 pm. As a result of this later end to the party the bus will go later, too, so it should read "Free transport to the student hostel is available leaving Blackwell House at 11:30". And of course other students may attend, and all students must have their student ID card with them.

I hope you can come to the welcoming party. It's a really good way to get to know other students and to learn what it's like to live in this city and to study here. Just one final change: please let us know by Thursday if you can come.

Narrator Now listen while Dave Burns gives instructions for students who are going to travel by car to the party. First look at questions 15 to 18. Write no more than three words for each answer.

Student Adviser Some of you may prefer to travel by car, but I have to warn you about some changes to the roads. You will find there is a lot of new road work on Smith Street. The work will not finish for a long time so we can be sure that Smith Street will be a problem.

If you are coming from the city you will be able to travel easily until you get to Blackwell Street, just near the college. As you know Blackwell Street is very long. You should avoid the corner of Blackwell Street and Jones Avenue, because they are laying telephone cable. However, you can take a detour and avoid Blackwell Street altogether. The best thing to do is to pass the roundabout and take the first road on your left which is Brown Crescent. Brown Crescent will lead you into the college grounds, so that's easy.

I hope everyone has a great time. Bring your friends, and we'll see you on Friday. Oh, one final reminder: it's best to use the side door. The front door may be locked at 7:00, so come to the side. See you on Friday.

Narrator That is the end of Section 2. You will now have some time to check your answers.

Now turn to Section 3.

Section 3. In this section you will hear a discussion between two students who have to describe a lawn sprinkler for part of their general science course. (A lawn sprinkler is a machine designed to water gardens and lawns). In the first part of the discussion the students are talking about the different parts of the sprinkler. First look at questions 19 to 23. Note the example that has been done for you.

Now listen to the conversation and label the parts of the sprinkler on the diagram. Choose from the box. There are more words in the box than you will need.

Linda Hello, Scott! I believe you're going to be my partner for this practical session. Have you got the model set up?

Scott Yes. Uh. It's right here. The instructions say we have to describe it first, and label the diagram. I've started from where the water enters the machine. Um. The water enters through a hose pipe and then it turns a water wheel. You can see where the wheel is marked by an arrow pointing upwards. It's called a water wheel because it's designed so the water will catch against the wheel. This action spins a series of gears ...

Linda How are you going to describe the gears?

Scott There are two worm gears, one vertical and one horizontal. The horizontal worm gear drives a circular gear. That gear is connected to a crank which changes the motion. The crank is already labelled. Do you see the two white arrows?

Linda I see. Okay, the water has passed across the water wheel. Then what?

Scott: Okay. Umm. Then you could say the water passes through the spray tube.

Linda Yes, I see.

Scott And the water is then spread over the lawn through holes at the top of the spray tube.

Linda How are you going to describe the base?

Scott How about this: "The sprinkler stands on a base consisting of two metal tubes which join at a hinge at one end and continue into a plastic moulding at the other."

Linda That's certainly starting at the bottom. Do you want to mention that there's no water in the base?

Scott I don't think that's necessary. If you look at the diagram it's easy to see that the only metal tube to contain water is the spray tube. You can actually see the water coming out of it.

Narrator Now listen while Linda and Scott's instructor, Mark Stewart, talks to them. Answer questions 24 to 29.

Mark Hello Scott, Linda. I'm glad I caught you before class. Did you know about the change in the examination schedule?

Scott Change?

Mark Yes. The last day of examinations for your group will be December 2nd instead of November 29th.

Scott Is that definite? We were told they'd be on November 26, and then there was a rumour they'd be on December the 1st.

Mark The schedule's gone to the printer. There can be no changes. It's definitely December 2nd.

Scott That's a relief. I'm going to the US on December the 4th.

Mark Are you one of the exchange students?

Scott Yeah. Yeah. I'm really looking forward to studying there. Do you know if their general science courses are anything like ours?

Linda It's not very likely.

Mark Actually, all basic general science courses are fairly similar. You'll find you're behind in some things and ahead in others. I wouldn't worry too much about the course. You've been doing well on this one. Linda, have you finished your assignment yet?

Linda I'm nearly there. I should be able to give it to you on Monday.

Mark That's good. I can't let you have another extension.

Linda I was really grateful for the extra time you gave me. That was a really big assignment.

Mark Well, I'll expect it next week. Now, would you like to hear the details of the timetable?

Scott Oh. Yes, please.

Mark I've just finished putting it on the noticeboard downstairs. Basically, you'll have four examinations. General mechanics is in the morning of December 1st, physics and maths are on the afternoon of the same day. Communications and English are on the morning of December 2nd, and Earth sciences in the afternoon.

Linda All over in two days!

Mark Yes. I'll miss teaching this class. You're all good at expressing your views, which makes for an interesting class. Some of the other first year classes won't talk, and they're rather boring to teach.

Narrator That is the end of Section 3. You will now have some time to check your answers.

Now turn to Section 4.

Section 4. You will hear an extract from a talk about student health, and specifically about ways to avoid headaches. Listen to what the speaker says, and complete the summary. First look at questions 30 to 40.

As you listen to the talk, answer questions 30 to 40. Complete the summary. Use words from the box. There are more words in the box than you need. Some words may be used more than once.

Broadcaster Hello. Welcome to the student orientation program. Today's session is on health issues, and this talk is about headaches, and how to avoid them. It may surprise you to hear that headaches are often caused by hunger! In fact one study suggested that 70% of headaches are related to hunger, which makes it the principal cause. The advice is simple: eat three meals a day and try to keep to a fairly regular schedule of meals.

People associate noise with headaches, and for most of us excessive noise creates the conditions for a headache. Very loud noise is unpleasant, and people usually remove themselves from it. Having said that, younger people tend to tolerate noise better than their elders, so I may be leaving noisy places far earlier than you. Just remember that exposure to too much noise may predispose you to a headache.

Of course, we all associate headaches with studying! In fact the headache probably doesn't come from the studying so much as from being tense. When we study hard, we often hunch over our work. Try raising your shoulders and tensing them—now relax. Can you feel how much more comfortable a relaxed stance is? Another thing—

it's very important to check that you are working in a good light. It will not actually hurt your eyes to work in a bad light, but it will make you tired very quickly and is very likely to give you a headache. What's more, if you have the book flat on a desk in front of you it will be harder to read, and you will have to hold your head at an odd angle. It is wise to have a bookrest which raises the material you are reading 45 degrees to the desk. This will help reduce your chance of a headache. Try to relax before bed so that you will be relaxed when you try to sleep—a soak in a hot bath may be helpful. It's also important to really sleep when you go to bed: a good mattress is a wise investment for people who want to avoid headaches.

This talk seems to keep coming back to tension. Tension may cause you to chew too forcefully, clench your jaw, or grind your teeth, and this in turn may lead to headaches. It is very easy to say that you shouldn't grind your teeth, and very hard to stop, particularly if you grind your teeth in your sleep. Try to avoid situations which will make you tense, particularly just before bed. If you do compulsively grind your teeth in your sleep, ask your dentist about a soft mouthguard.

In general, try to eat regular meals and avoid tense situations. Be sure you get plenty of exercise. Hopefully your headaches will be greatly reduced. One other thing I should point out—avoid smoky rooms and cars. Such places certainly encourage headaches, and the smoke may be doing you quite serious long-term damage.

Narrator That is the end of Section 4. Now you have some time to check your answers.

That is the end of Test 4.

SECTION ONE

1 A
2 B
3 D
4 A
5 D
6 C
7 A
8 3
9 5

SECTION TWO

10 8:25 (am)
11 coach
12 2
13 Friday
14 (sailing) boat
15 (Greek) music
16 B; D
17 A; B
18 B; D
19 Greek tour
20 AA3 (not aa3)

SECTION THREE

21 1987
22 Turkey
23 English for farming
24 16 weeks / 4 months
25 14 (students)
26 former / previous / old students
27 all (students)
28 all (students)
28 advanced (students)
30 all (students)
31 beginners

SECTION FOUR

32 A
33 C
34 B
35 D
36 B
37 A
38 Social life
39 Hide (extra) fees
40 The government

Narrator Prepare for IELTS Practice Listening Tests. Practice Listening Test 5. Turn to Section 1 of Practice Listening Test 5.

Section 1. Megan and Ken are deciding how they will spend the evening. Look at section 1 of your listening test. You have some time to look at Questions 1 to 7 now. You will see that there is an example which has been done for you. The conversation relating to this will be played first.

Telephone rings

Megan Hello. Megan speaking.

Ken Hello Megan.

Megan Hello Ken. I'm glad you called. Thomas asked me to give you his telephone number.

Ken Is that his office number or his home number?

Megan I can give you both. His new home number is 9452 3456. Would you like his office number?

Ken I think I have it. Does 9731 4322 sound right?

Megan That's it. But the home number is 9452 3456. He moved in last week.

Ken Good. I've got that. Now, what would you like to do?

Narrator Thomas's home telephone number is 9452 3456 so letter C has been circled. Now we shall begin. You should answer the recording as you listen because you will not hear the questions a second time. First, you have another chance to look at questions 1 to 7. Now listen carefully and answer questions 1 to 7.

Telephone rings

Megan Hello. Megan speaking.

Ken Hello Megan.

Megan Hello Ken. I'm glad you called. Thomas asked me to give you his telephone number.

Ken Is that his office number or his home number?

Megan I can give you both. His new home number is 9452 3456. Would you like his office number?

Ken I think I have it. Does 9731 4322 sound right?

Megan That's it. But the home number is 9452 3456. He moved in last week.

Ken Good. I've got that. Now, what would you like to do?

Megan Well, I'd like to go dancing, but Jane's hurt her ankle so she'd rather not.

Ken That's a pity. I guess it means she doesn't want to play tennis, either.

Megan That's right. She says it's okay to go bowling if we don't expect her to do well.

Ken Okay, let's do it! I guess we can go dancing another time.

Megan Well, I booked us some time at the bowling alley of Entertainment City. Do you know it?

Ken Is it on Smith Street, down near the university?

Megan That's right. It's on the corner of Smith Street and Bridge Road.

Ken What time did you book for?

Megan The first booking I could get was eight o'clock.

Ken Okay. It's seven now. What do you want to do first?

Megan Well, I think we should leave now. We can meet at the bowling alley.

Ken I can't be that quick. I have to call Thomas, to start with, and I need to get changed.

Megan Okay. I think I'll leave in 10 minutes and meet you in there.

Ken That makes sense. I'll take my car, so I'll be quite quick. I'll be out of here in half an hour.

Megan Okay. You're so lucky to have a car! You can get around so easily.

Ken Well, yes and no. I often spend ages driving around trying to find a park. The traffic can be very bad.

Megan Well, that won't be a problem for me, because I'll take the bus. It goes right past my door, and I'll have plenty of time.

Ken Sounds good. Who else is coming?

Megan I think nearly everyone from the afternoon class will be there.

Ken Which class? The big maths class, or the afternoon tutorial?

Megan The maths class. What's more, we get a concession for large numbers!

Ken That's good. I'm trying to keep my expenses down this month.

Megan So am I. I expect tonight'll cost about $20.

Ken You must be good with money. I expect it to come to ... um ... nearly $40! So how are you going to manage that?

Megan Well, the bus is cheap, and if I come home early I won't have time to spend too much! In any case, I have to be up early tomorrow morning, so I'd really better try to get home by about 11.

Ken That reminds me. I have to phone the taxi company for my mother. Goodbye, Megan. I'll see you later.

Megan: Goodbye, Ken.

Sound of phone hanging up.

Narrator: Ken calls the taxi company. Now listen to the telephone call and be ready to answer questions 8 and 9.

Sound of somebody dialling, phone ringing

Man's voice Hello, this is Acme Cabs. Please follow the instructions on the tape.

If you wish to order a cab now, press 1.

If you have placed an order previously, press 2.

If you wish to make an advance order, Press 3. Please be ready to tell us your street number and name.

If you wish to speak to the radio room supervisor, press 4.

If you want to enquire about lost property, press 5.

If you want to order a taxi equipped to carry wheelchairs, press 6.

Your call is very important. Please stay on the line for the next available order taker.

Click to indicate a real person is there.

Ken Hello. I think I left something in one of your cabs on Thursday. It was a brown paper package with an address written on it in green ink. Has anyone handed it in?

Narrator That is the end of Section 1. You now have some time to check your answers.

Now turn to Section 2.

Section 2. You are going to hear some announcements made to a group of people who are planning a trip to Greece. First look at questions 10 to 15. As you listen to the first part of the talk answer questions 10 to 15. Write no more than three words or numbers for each answer.

Tour organiser Good morning everyone. I'm getting very excited about this trip to Greece, and I'm sure you are too. As you know, we didn't have all the details at our last meeting, but I can give them to you now.

We'll leave London Gatwick Airport on British Airways next Wednesday. Please be sure to be at the airport by 6:30. I know it's early, but our departure time is 8:25am. We're quite a large group, and we don't want to have any hassles. Please be sure to have all your travel documents ready. We'll arrive in Athens at 2:25 in the afternoon, and there'll be a vehicle there to meet us. It'll be a full-sized coach so everyone can travel together.

We'll spend three full days in our hotel in Athens, although we're only being charged for two nights' accommodation, which is good news. The second day we'll go to the National Archaeological Museum to see the enormous collection of ancient Greek works of art, antiques, statues—a brilliant display. We'll eat out at a typical Greek restaurant on Thursday night. It's going to be a very busy time in Athens! Friday morning and afternoon we'll visit historic sites, but we have nothing planned for the rest of the day.

On Saturday we're off to the islands, the Greek islands of ancient myth and modern romance. Now, the big news! At first we thought we'd take the ferry, but we've been very lucky to secure a sailing boat which is big enough for all of us. I'm really excited about this part of the trip, because we'll see the islands to the best advantage, and we'll be able to cruise around and sleep on board. We'll get off at different islands and for one part of the trip we'll have people playing Greek traditional music actually on board with us. Now I'll pass out a brochure with all the details.

Narrator Now look at questions 16 to 18. As the talk continues answer questions 16 to 18.

Tour organiser A lot of work has gone into organising this tour, and I'd like to thank in particular the travel agent who got us a really good deal and the people at the British Museum who offered us such good advice. Trips like this only happen because of the hard work of really expert people.

As you know, we have planned a gathering for when we return. I have a list of things which the committee would like you to bring to the party. They are: your pictures and something to eat for everyone to share.

You are almost bound to have people ask what we have in common, and why we are travelling as a group. I suppose the answer is that we are interested in learning about old societies and vanished cultures, and we all enjoy travelling. Of course, we enjoy fine food too, but that's not as important!

Narrator Now look at questions 19 and 20. As the talk continues answer questions 19 and 20.

Tour organiser I nearly forgot the last piece of information. You will see there are labels which I have passed around for you to put on all your luggage. Could you fill them in, please? On the top line please write "Greek tour" and on the lower line, write, in block letters, I mean upper case, the letters AA and the number 3—that's AA3.

We need to have these labels clearly displayed to help the baggage handlers keep our luggage together on the different parts of our trip, so please don't take them off.

Narrator That is the end of section 2. You now have some time to check your answers. Now turn to section 3.

Section 3. You are going to hear Dr Joanne Robinson, the course director of a Language Learning Centre, answering questions from reporters from the student newspaper. First look at questions 21 to 26. As you listen to the first part of the talk, answer questions 21 to 26. Write no more than three words or numbers for each answer.

Course Director Welcome to the Language Learning Centre. I'm Joanne Robinson. You must be the reporters from The Examiner. Please come in and sit down.

Cheryl Hello Dr Robinson. Yes, we're from The Examiner. I'm Cheryl Perkins and this is Don Klim. May I start with a question? Did this college really start with Brazilian students?

Course Director It did. The Language Learning Centre was founded in 1985 to look after a group of students from Brazil who wanted to study here. Those twenty students soon grew

to 60, and, as you can imagine, we had severe accommodation problems.

Don Somebody said you were in the old amenities block, right near the engineering school.

Course Director They have a good memory! Yes, we were there, because the university hadn't believed we would expand so quickly. The problem wasn't solved until we moved into these new premises in Bancroft House in 1987.

Don When did you start taking students from other countries?

Course Director About 1990. We now have students from 13 different countries enrolled, and we expect a large group from Turkey next month.

Cheryl Yes, we've noticed a lot more advertisements for Turkish restaurants in our advertising section.

Course Director Well, 40% of our students come from Turkey, by far the largest single national group, and I believe there's been an influx to the rest of the university. There are a lot of Turkish students studying hospitality.

Cheryl Do you offer anything special to the students?

Course Director Yes, we do. There are several things which make us rather different from other language schools. English is certainly not restricted to English for academic purposes here! Sometimes we have extra classes for students who have particular courses in mind, and we have just said goodbye to a group of thirty Indonesian students who were preparing for a university course in agriculture. They came to us for English for farming, and they were with us for a long time. We miss them!

Cheryl How long do students usually stay at the Language Learning Centre?

Course Director It varies, so I'll talk about the average. Most of our courses last for five weeks, but to make any real progress a student needs to be here for at least three terms, that's fifteen weeks. The students do better if they have a little time to settle in at the beginning of the course, and we offer an orientation course that lasts a week. Most students take it. It helps them to settle down, and it gives us plenty of time to test them and place them at the right level.

Don How many people are in each class?

Course Director We sometimes go up to 18, but our average class size is 14 students, and some classes have as few as seven participants. It depends on the needs of the group.

Cheryl You were saying that you miss your students when they go. How do you attract students? I mean, how do they hear about the Language Learning Centre in the first place?

Course Director We're included in the university advertising and marketing, and we have our own website. The thing which works best for us, though, is word of mouth. Students who leave us often send us their friends. In fact, a student who arrived today was carrying a photograph for me of a former student and his baby!

Cheryl It sounds like a nice place to be!

Course Director It is! A lot of our students make lasting friendships while they're here.

Narrator Now look at questions 27 to 31. As the talk continues, answer questions 27 to 31.

Cheryl Making friends with other students sounds special enough! I'd like to emphasise that in the student newspaper.

Course Director We do try to get our students to be part of the wider university.

Don How do you do that? Do you encourage them to join the Sports Centre, for instance?

Course Director Indeed we do! The Sports Centre is always looking for active participants, particularly in soccer. Oh, and something else. You might like to mention that we don't teach just English here. I mean, we're a language centre, not an English language centre. You may learn Spanish, Mandarin, and Russian here, and we can sometimes offer other languages. This means we can have some students who are native speakers of those languages as conversation partners for English-speaking students.

Cheryl Who can do those courses?

Course Director At this time, any native speaker of English.

Cheryl What about the people who are learning English? Can they do a non-English language course?

Course Director At this time, only if they've almost finished their English language course. You see, we try very hard to involve students who are native speakers of English as conversation leaders and we encourage our students to join groups on the campus. For instance, if they enjoy music, there is an active jazz group available to everyone, and that's a lot of fun. On the other hand, elementary students can't go to the drama group, their English just isn't ready for that sort of activity, but the university choir welcomes all the singers it can find. They often do large productions that need a lot of voices.

Cheryl I imagine the special conversation groups are open to all your students ...

Course Director I wish they were. I'm sorry to say they're a special service we provide for elementary students only. Is there anything else I can tell you? **(pause)** I'd be really pleased if you could write about the courses we offer in foreign languages.

Cheryl I think our readers would be very interested in that. Thank you for your time, Dr Robinson.

Don Yes, thank you very much.

Course Director Goodbye. Thank you for giving me the opportunity to talk about the centre. It's always good to let the rest of the students at the university know what goes on in our classrooms, and outside them! After all, many of our students leave us and then study for degrees in various disciplines on this campus.

Narrator That is the end of Section 3. You will now have some time to check your answers. Now turn to Section 4.

Section 4. You will hear a talk about the pitfalls and pleasures of being a postgraduate student.

Look at questions 32 to 37. Listen to the speaker's advice and answer questions 32 to 37. Circle the correct letter.

Speaker Postgraduates are about as easy to define as catching steam in a bucket. Courses can be vocational, for training, as research, as a preparation for research, or a combination of these. Also you can choose between full-time and part-time. Increasingly, the approach to postgraduate study is becoming modular. The vast majority of postgraduates are doing short, taught courses, many of which provide specific vocational training. Indeed, there has been a 400% increase in postgraduate numbers in Britain over the past 20 years. Current figures stand at just under 400,000.

People undertake postgraduate study for many reasons. These may be academic (intellectual challenge, development of knowledge), vocational (training for a specific career goal) or only vague (drifting into further study). It is essential that you determine the reasons you want to become a postgraduate. If you have clear goals and reasons for studying, this will enhance your learning experience and help you to remain focused and motivated throughout your course.

Where you study should be based on much more than the course you want to do. For some courses you are likely to be there for several years, and it is important that you are happy living there. Check also what type of accommodation is available and whether the institution provides any housing specifically for postgraduates.

Choosing an institution and department is a difficult process. To determine quality, do not rely on the reputation of an institution, but find out what ratings are from the most recent assessment exercises. Find out about the staff, their reputation, competence, enthusiasm and friendliness. Visit the department if possible and talk to existing postgraduates about their experience, satisfaction, comments and complaints. Be very careful to check how they feel about their supervisors.

Also, check what facilities are available, both at an institutional level (for example libraries, laboratory and computing facilities) and in the department (for example study room, desk, photocopying, secretarial support etc).

Everyone will have their own priorities here: I am always anxious to check the computer support available, and regard it as slightly more important than library access. Your working environment and the support available to you plays an essential part in making your work as a postgraduate a positive experience.

Life as a postgraduate can be very different to your other experiences of education. Things that can distinguish your experience are the level of study, independence of working, intensity of the course, the demands on your time, and often the fact that you are older than the majority of the students.

These factors can contribute to making you feel isolated. However, there are several ways you can make sure that this is either short-lived or does not happen at all.

Many student unions have postgraduate societies that organise social events and may also provide representation for postgraduates to both the student union and the institution. Departments can also help to create a sense of identity and community, and often have discussion groups available. Don't be afraid to talk to staff about any difficulties you might be having. Of course universities provide counselling services but we have found that the best advice comes from talking to other postgraduates who may have faced similar difficulties.

Narrator Look at questions 38 to 40. Write no more than three words or numbers for each answer.

Speaker Financial planning is essential, since the government excludes postgraduates from student loans, and it can be difficult to maintain your student status with banks. This has implications for free banking and overdraft facilities. Do not underestimate your living costs, including food, accommodation and travel, and be careful not to budget for everything except a social life.

Funding a course is one of the most challenging things people face when considering postgraduate study. Most postgraduate students are self-financing. They pay (often very large) fees to the institution and receive no maintenance income to support their study. Make sure you know exactly what your costs will be—institutions often hide extra fees like laboratory costs behind the headline fee rate advertised.

Funding can come from various sources. Research councils, charities, trust funds, institutional scholarships, local education authorities and professional bodies and organisations all offer various levels of funding. As I said before, the government excludes postgraduates from student loans, so it is essential you look to other sources. Career development loans are available from high street banks. The best advice on funding is to be proactive, persistent and patient.

The postgraduate community in Britain is multinational, has a wide range of experience of life and work and an exciting mix of goals, both career and academic. Being a postgraduate student should be a productive and fulfilling thing to do, and you will become part of a diverse and motivated social group.

Narrator That is the end of Section 4. You now have some time to check your answers.

That is the end of Listening Practice Test 5.

ANSWER KEY
Reading **Test 1**

ANSWER KEY
Reading **Test 2**

ANSWER KEY
Reading **Test 3**

SECTION ONE
1 18
2 28, 33
   (must have both answers;
   the question says "two
   pages"; page 30 is not
   correct as the question asks
   about "art" not "the arts")
3 32
   (the sports stadium is
   discussed in the "Letters"
   page)
4 monthly / every month /
   each month
5 A
6 C
7 A,E (must have both
   answers)
8 E
9 B
10 D
11 C
12 A
13 B
14 D
    (note the importance of the
    article "the" i.e. "the snake"
    that has bitten you, not
    snakes in general)
15 B

SECTION TWO
Student Accommodation at
Northside University
16 C
17 B
18 A
19 B
20 $68.50
21 $154
    (the answer requires "the
    cheapest" not the range)
22 21
23 17
24 Boronia
25 women

SECTION THREE
Kormilda College
26 1969
27 280
28 D
29 pre-secondary
30 supported secondary
31 secondary
32 English
33 science
34 T
35 NG
36 F
37 NG
38 T
39 NG
40 T

SECTION ONE
1 E
2 B & C
3 D
4 A
5 D
6 C
7 R
8 E
9 R
10 CP
11 R
12 CP
13 birdsong
14 binoculars
15 (billy) tea, damper
    (must have both)
16 Possum Prowl
17 non-slip shoes
18 (lovely) (water) views

SECTION TWO
Community College Courses
19 VII
20 IV
21 I
22 III
23 II
24 A
25 E
26 B & C
27 D
28 D
29 communication

SECTION THREE
Great Inventions
30 C
31 C
32 D
33 A
34 B
35 D
36 F
37 NG
38 T
39 T
40 F

SECTION ONE
1 1821
2 (The) Hunter (River)
3 1870
4 A & C
5 B
6 A
7 D
8 I
9 G
10 K
11 J
12 E
13 H
14 F

SECTION TWO
Numeracy Centre
15 free
16 lecture
17 9
18 tutorial
19 Course B / Statistics for
    Marketing
20 workshops
21 $15
22 workshops and notes
23 D
24 A
25 N
26 C
27 B

SECTION THREE
Business Planning
28 Yes
29 No
30 Not Given
    (even though the plan is
    comprehensive,
    it cannot be argued that
    by implication the answer
    would be 'No')
31 Yes
    ("the key question to ask")
32 Yes
33 Yes
34 No
35 C
36 J
37 I
38 F or H
39 H or F
40 B

READING

SECTION ONE
1 E
2 A
3 C
4 C
5 H
6 I
7 M
8 hh:mm
9 (Daily) Work Record
10 (your/the) supervisor
11 Monday
12 (your) Tax Number
13 your / the employee's home
   address

SECTION TWO
Language and Culture
Centre
14 pool, table tennis
   (must have both answers)
15 international clubs
16 University Health Centre
17 Health Insurance
18 (a weather) emergency
   / emergency weather
   conditions
19 15 minutes
20 50%
21 D
22 C
23 A
24 B
25 D
26 A
27 B

SECTION THREE
Employment in Japan
28 E
29 G
30 B
31 A
32 H
33 D
34 F
35 I
36 loyalty
37 twice yearly / twice a year
38 mentor
39 B
40 B

SECTION ONE
1 Developmental art
2 $4.50
3 Developmental art
4 $5.00
5 North Gallery
6 New Year festivities
7 632
8 132
9 317
10 122
11 443
12 C; H
13 D; G
14 A
15 B

SECTION TWO
Language Resource Centre
16 Language Centre students
17 Photo-ID card
18 (in) cash
19 REF in red
20 IELTS (materials)
21 False
22 False
23 Not Given
24 True
25 False
26 Not Given
27 True
28 Not Given

SECTION THREE
How Babies learn Language
29 language development
30 3 or 4; 3-4 years
31 models
32 exaggerate
33 recognise
34 conversation / interaction /
   communication
35 Yes
36 Yes
37 Yes
38 Not Give
39 No
40 No

TEXT ONE
Australia's Linguistic History
1 1850s (paragraph 2)
2 1901 (paragraph 2)
3 1891 (paragraph 2)
4 1946 (paragraph 3: 'the period from 1900 to 1946 saw the consolidation of the English language in Australia').
5 1971 (paragraph 5: 'between 1947 and 1971...')
6 1973 (paragraph 4: 'Since 1973, Australian immigration policies have not discriminated against people on the grounds of race...')

TEXT TWO
The Composition of Australia's Overseas-Born Population by Birthplace
1 Europe
2 Italy (footnote 1: To add the USSR here is incorrect; the figures for Europe include the USSR but the USSR was not one of the principal source countries for immigrants)
3 Asia
4 Vietnam (footnote 2)
5 Turkey (footnote 2)
6 Middle East
7 New Zealand
8 45 (footnote 4: 45% of the African total were from South Africa)

TEXT THREE
Optimum Age for Language Learning
1 level
('examination' is not logical)
2 optimum
('optimum' = best; the 'however' at the beginning of the sentence clearly shows that an opposite point of view to the previous sentence is about to be stated)
3 acquire
(the space needs an infinitive verb)
4 worst
('early adolescence' reminds the reader that secondary school language teaching is being discussed, and the use of 'in fact' gives emphasis to this opposing view that is being expressed)
5 emotional
('given' here means 'if we take into account'; that is, if we consider the problems of teenagers we would realise that adolescence is not a good time for the extra stress of learning a language)
6 no
(that is, one can learn a language at any age: note the double negative)
7 accent
(clear from the next sentence)
8 debated
('controversy' is not possible here; the space needs a past participle to complete the verb).

TEXT FOUR
The Heat Is On
1 Prediction No. 2
2 Prediction No. 1
3 Prediction No. 3
4 Prediction No. 4
5 India
6 December 1998
7 September 1998
8 Turkey
9 Philippines

TEXT FIVE
General Information for Students
1 A
2 B
3 B
4 C
5 C (compare 'Student ID cards' and 'Movie Concession pass')
6 B
7 C

TEXT SIX
Positions Vacant
1 9444 3331
2 write a letter
3 9776 5489
4 driver's licence
5 (names of) two referees

TEXT SEVEN
Consumer Bookshelf
1 Book Number 3
2 Book Number 6
3 Book Number 4
4 Book Number 7
5 Book Number 5
6 Book Number 1

TEXT EIGHT
TAFE Courses
1 5418
2 3103
3 3519
4 3534
5 8510
6 0843
7 0842
8 5419

TEXT NINE
Course Information Evenings
1 D
2 A

TEXT TEN
Dial-It Information Services
1 11680
2 1196
3 11540
4 11511
5 11640

TASK 1
SUGGESTED APPROACH

The answer should describe an event which is in the news, and explain why people are interested. You do not need to worry if your information about the news is not accurate. You are being assessed on the way you write your answer, not on whether what you write is true.

SAMPLE ANSWER

Dear _____

How are you? The last time you wrote you asked about local news items, so I thought I'd fill you in on how Australia has been affected by the horrific tsunami which devastated so many countries around the Indian Ocean.

We first heard the shocking news on Boxing Day (26 December) but no one realised the extent of the damage or the human toll. It was such an unusual event, something one would only expect to see in a Hollywood film. Australia was affected because we are part of this region, geographically and politically.

Australia has close ties with Indonesia and Thailand, so we are focusing our aid chiefly on those countries. Our Foreign Minister is there now surveying the damage and key divisions of the Australian army are helping in Indonesia.

A friend of mine is the manager of one of the large resorts in Phuket – the one which was completely inundated. Fortunately, he was holidaying in Europe at the time! Many other Australians were not so lucky.

Trust you are well. Write soon.

_____

177 words

TASK 2
SUGGESTED APPROACH

The answer should explain clearly what people do to stay healthy in your country. Relate your answer to diet, exercise and the avoidance of stress.

SAMPLE ANSWER

These days people are becoming more concerned with remaining healthy and avoiding illness. There are several ways people stay healthy in my country, Australia. Basically, these can be divided into what we eat, getting enough exercise and rest, and then remaining calm.

Most Australians understand that it is necessary to eat well and eat regularly. Having three good meals a day and actually taking time to eat properly is important. This means trying to have a balanced diet of protein (fish, meat, eggs) and vegetables and fruit, for breakfast, lunch and dinner.

It is sometimes difficult to find time to exercise every day, but if we can manage a few days a week when we find time to get some physical exercise, then we will feel better for it. We will also sleep more soundly and peacefully. Australians enjoy outdoor sports, swimming and cricket in summer, and football in winter.

Many Australians relax by walking or even, these days, practising yoga. Relaxing helps us to remain calm and reduce stress. The best way of reducing stress, however, is to understand what is causing it. If we have too many things to do, it is best to make a list, and then to organise what we have to do according to how important each thing is. Taking control is the best way to lower anxiety levels.

So, in Australia, with our wonderful climate and the availability of good fresh food it is not difficult to stay healthy. By taking control of our lives and planning, we will all feel less stressed.

260 words

TASK 1
SUGGESTED APPROACH
The answer should explain why you are dissatisfied, and what you expect the restaurant to do.

SAMPLE ANSWER
Dear Sir/Madam

I am the club secretary for the North Sydney football club. Every month the club committee meets, and following this meeting we have dinner at your restaurant. I regret to say that last Friday the meal we had was unsatisfactory, both in terms of the quality of the food and the service.

There were several problems with the food last Friday. Some of the orders were overcooked, and one was completely burnt. The salads were definitely not fresh! For example, the lettuce was either white or brown and definitely not crisp or green.

The service that evening was also not up to your usual standard. We have never experienced such a long delay. The waiter did not explain or apologise, and did nothing to repair the problem. He might have offered a complimentary drink or something.

Before the club committee would consider returning to your restaurant we would need some assurance that the food will be fresh and that the service will be courteous and professional.

Yours faithfully

_____

168 words

TASK 2
SUGGESTED APPROACH
The answer should talk about acceptable behaviour for children in different cultures, and explain what factors help adults to decide what is acceptable behaviour.

SAMPLE ANSWER
Childhood is the time of learning for children. Different countries have different rules of behaviour, but if children do not learn the correct rules they may not be able to fit into their society when they grow up. I believe it is important for children to learn that they must follow certain rules in their society.

Different countries have their own ideas about what is polite and acceptable behaviour. In some societies at school children are expected to remain quiet, and pay close attention to the teacher. It is considered very impolite for a student to ask questions and interrupt a teacher. However, in other societies it is not only considered acceptable behaviour, but children are encouraged to ask teachers questions.

What is acceptable behaviour for children is determined by the traditions and customs of a country. Even though these traditions and customs differ from country to country, all adults naturally want their children to grow up to be respectful citizens in their country. Being different does not mean being wrong. It is simply the responsibility of parents to teach their society's accepted code of behaviour to their children.

In conclusion, although each country has different ideas about acceptable behaviour for children, I believe that it is important for children to learn exactly what is acceptable and what is not. This should be done by parents laying down appropriate rules and then taking responsibility for ensuring that their children follow them.

241 words

TASK 1
SUGGESTED APPROACH
The answer should explain your special circumstances. It should give reasons why the Enrolment Officer should make an exception for you.

SAMPLE ANSWER
Dear Sir/Madam

I am particularly interested in enrolling in the computer course which is being offered at your college. I noticed the advertisement in the local newspaper, and I noted that the course is for those who have formal training in computing at college or university level.

I have not done any formal study in computing. I am writing to ask if you would make an exception to your course entry requirements based on my background reading and the level of computer skills I have developed.

Computers are my passion and I have built up an extensive computer reference library. I subscribe to several computer magazines. I have taught myself all major computer languages, including Cobalt and Fortran. I am familiar with most computer software applications for word processing, spreadsheets and databases, as well as websites.

I am available for an interview, as well as a placement test so that I can demonstrate both my knowledge and skills.

I hope you will consider my request favourably.

Yours faithfully,

166 words

TASK 2
SUGGESTED APPROACH
The answer should identify the difficulties of a particular country. The answer should describe the problem(s) and suggest how it/they can be overcome.

SAMPLE ANSWER
As economies develop and the world's population grows, the countries of the world have to tackle new and complicated issues. Over the next ten years Australia will have to deal with several critical problems, such as the environment, its infrastructure and access to education.

Water, air and land are all affected by pollution, whether it is caused by human waste or chemicals in the emissions and effluent from factories and vehicles. Over-watering because of extensive irrigation and the use of chemical fertilisers on farms is also degrading our land. Overcrowding and poor design of internal and public space leads to significant levels of noise pollution. Everyone wants cleaner water and air, and we certainly need quality land and soil to grow the food we need.

As cities grow and become more crowded so we need to travel further to work and then home again. Quality and standards are being raised all the time —faster and safer freeways and transport systems, more comfortable travel with air-conditioning and softer seating.

Education and training is becoming more critically important. It is expected that increasing numbers of highly educated and trained recruits will be needed in the workforce. Companies are looking to employ applicants with postgraduate qualifications, so no longer are undergraduate degrees sufficient.

The cost of providing and maintaining healthy environments, transport and extended education options is enormous. Governments are now forcing the public, those who use our natural resources to pay by levying water, fining factories which pollute rivers and the atmosphere, and raising transport fares. Education is also becoming more expensive.

260 words

TASK 1
SUGGESTED APPROACH
The answer should explain how you lost your card yesterday, so the explanation will be in the past tense. It should include a request for a new card, and an explanation of why the card is important to you.

SAMPLE ANSWER
Dear Sir/Madam

I am writing to advise you that I lost my student identification card yesterday and to ask for a new card to be issued as quickly as possible. There are several reasons why I need a new card by the end of this week.

I live in the outer suburbs and depend on both trains and buses to get to class every day. I also need a student card to be able to borrow library books to complete my assignments. Less importantly, I cannot afford to go to the cinema unless I have a student discount. Again, I need the card for that.

Most importantly, however, I use this card as proof of identification when withdrawing money from the bank. This week I have to pay rent for next month and will have to withdraw a large amount of money to cover this. I pay the rent by bank cheque.

I apologise for any inconvenience caused.

Yours faithfully,

_____

158 words

TASK 2
SUGGESTED APPROACH
The answer should give sensible arguments for why there is poverty, and offer suggestions on ways to help the poor.

SAMPLE ANSWER
Even in developed countries a degree of poverty exists. However, in many developing countries poverty is a major problem, and the number of poor people continues to increase. There are various factors that cause poverty and these need to be addressed to help the poor.

The first factor influencing world poverty is the current global economic system. This system reinforces inequality between rich and poor people since it allows resources to be distributed unequally amongst people. In addition, the global economic system can favour the investment strategies of large transnational corporations, which often pay their workers sub-standard wages.

Another reason for world poverty is illiteracy. Many people around the world do not have access to education, and as a result do not learn to read or write. They are, therefore, precluded from well-paid employment and so can not improve their living conditions.

In order to provide help for the world's poor these problems need to be addressed. Firstly, the international community has to establish a fairer economic system in which the wealth of each country can be shared equitably amongst its people. Moreover, all countries around the world should make it a priority to eradicate illiteracy by providing comprehensive education for all citizens so that everyone is equally capable of improving their living standards via access to education.

To conclude, it can be said that poverty will probably always exist. Nevertheless, countries around the world can take actions to reduce poverty by ensuring that there is a fair distribution of wealth amongst people, and by making sure that all people have access to education.

267 words

TASK 1
SUGGESTED APPROACH
The answer should complain about the bus service and give details of the bad parts of the service. The answer should tell the bus company what you expect them to do about the problem.

SAMPLE ANSWER
Dear Sir/Madam,

I am a regular passenger on the 388 bus service. I have always found it to be a good service both punctual and clean. However, over the last two weeks this situation has changed. The 388 is no longer reliable and it is dirty.

The bus now arrives behind schedule. For example, on the 16th and 17th November the bus that was scheduled to arrive at Springwood Street at 8.30am arrived at 8.40am. Then, on 21st, 22nd and 23rd November the bus was not only late, but it failed to stop as well.

In addition, the bus is no longer as clean as it previously was. I have noticed papers and bottles down the aisle and under seats.

The deterioration of the 388 bus service is unacceptable, and I request that you do everything possible to return the service to its former punctual and clean level.

I look forward to your swift attention to this matter.

Yours faithfully,

156 words

TASK 2
SUGGESTED APPROACH
The answer should give suggestions on how a health service should be organised.

SAMPLE ANSWER
Access to a reliable and good quality health service is important for the people of any country. Developments in medical treatment and medical technology over the last few decades have seen the costs of health care rise making it unaffordable to many people in the community. There are two reasons why a free health service should be available to all, namely the high cost of treatment and the government's duty to its people.

Firstly, without government provision of free health care, the less advantaged members of the community, such as the unemployed and the aged, would not be able to afford medical treatment. This situation would result in great suffering and further entrench the disadvantaged status of these groups. Secondly, the purpose of any government is to ensure the wellbeing of its people. By providing a free health care service, the government would be directly attending to this duty.

The health care service should be organised in a way that caters for the needs of the population as a whole. This means that the government must prioritise medical services. For example, there could be provision for free access to consultation with doctors as well as free access to general hospital care. On the other hand, free access to more expensive and specialised treatments may need to have some restrictions due to the high costs involved.

In conclusion, free health care of a good overall quality is an important service for a government to provide because it has a duty to ensure that all people in the community are taken care of.

261 words

TRANSCRIPTS
Practice **Speaking Tests**

Transcripts of the Sample Speaking Interviews can be downloaded by visiting www.insearch.edu.au

ANSWERS & TRANSCRIPTS
WRITING